SKILLS IN RELIGIOUS STUDIES

Book 1

J FAGEANT AND S C MERCIER

Heinemann

Heinemann Educational Publishers
Halley Court, Jordan Hill, Oxford OX2 8EJ
a division of Reed Educational & Professional Publishing Ltd

OXFORD PORTSMOUTH NH (USA) CHICAGO
MELBOURNE AUCKLAND IBADAN
GABORONE JOHANNESBURG BLANTYRE

Heinemann is a registered trademark of Reed Educational &
Professional Publishing Ltd

Text © J Fageant and S C Mercier, 1997

First published 1987
This edition published 1997

02 01 00
10 9 8 7 6 5 4 3

British Library Cataloguing in Publication Data
A catalogue record for this book is available from the
British Library

ISBN 0 435 30203 5

Designed and typeset by Ken Vail Graphic Design, Cambridge
Picture research by Jacqui Rivers
Cover designed by Aricot Vert
Printed and bound in Great Britain by Bath Colourbooks, Glasgow

Acknowledgements

The publishers would like to thank the following for
permission to reproduce copyright material.
David Campbell Publishers for the quote from *Hindu
Scriptures*, trans. Zaehner RC, 1966 on p. 12; By
permission of Oxford University Press the quote from
Bhagavad Gita, trans. Zaehner RC, 1969 on p. 15;
Scriptures quoted from the *Good News Bible* published
by the Bible Societies/HarperCollins Publishers Ltd.,
UK, © American Bible Society, 1966, 1971, 1976, 1992
on pp. 22, 23, 24, 54; The Muslim Educational Trust for
the diagram and quotes on pp. 65, 67 and 70 from
Islam: Beliefs and Teachings by Ghulam Sarwar, 1992;
The Guardian for the headline on p. 67; The *Independent*
for the material on p. 67; Reprinted with permission of
India Book House Limited, Mumbai, the publishers of
Amar Chitra Katha, the material on p. 80; The Sikh
Missionary Society for the Mool Mantar on p. 82.

The publishers would like to thank the following for
permission to use photographs.
Andes Press Agency p. 58; Barnaby's Picture Library p.
59; Robin Bath pp. 35, 43, 46; Bridgeman Art Library
pp. 6, 15; Circa Photo Library pp. 7, 9, 12, 13, 21, 26,
30, 31, 48, 56, 70, 79, 84, 85, 91, 93; John Crook p. 61;
Eye Ubiquitous pp. 25, 54, 57, 62, 90; Josephine
Fageant p. 59; Format Photographers pp. 31 (Brenda
Prince), 89 (Judy Harrison); Sally and Richard
Greenhill p. 7; Sonia Halliday pp. 62, 64; Hutchison
Photo Library pp. 18, 20, 32, 33, 42, 49, 53, 69; Impact
Photo Library pp. 10 (Mark Henley) 35, 50 (Mohamed
Ansar), 52 (David Reed), 69, 82, 93; London Buddhist
Centre p. 43; Network Photographers p. 51 (Barrie
Lewis); Panos pp. 4, 24, 36, 45, 49, 53; Ann and Bury
Peerless pp. 8, 16, 38, 39, 40, 45, 47, 68, 92; Popperfoto
pp. 5, 57, 63, 71; Peter Sanders Photographer pp. 11,
22, 55, 71, 73, 74, 75, 76, 77; Juliette Soester pp. 22, 23,
26, 28, 29; Barry Stone p. 33; Tony Stone p. 24; Trip
pp. 17 (Dinodia), 19 (B. Turner), 37 (J. Wakelin), 41
(Eric Smith), 44 (N. Ray), 46 (F. Good), 60, 61, 66, 72,
81, 86, 87 (H. Rogers); Tropix/Veronica Birley p. 51;
Twin Studio pp. 78, 83.

The publishers would like to thank CIRCA Photo
Library/Twin Studio, Eye Ubiquitous/Paul Seheult,
Panos Pictures/Anna Tully, Peter Sanders, Tony Stone
Images and Zefa Picture Library for permission to
reproduce the cover photographs.

The publishers have made every effort to trace
copyright holders. However, if any material has been
incorrectly acknowledged, we would be pleased to
correct this at the earliest opportunity.

Contents

1 Learning about religions

Young people in the UK probably know more about different religions than young people in most other countries in the world. In many places there is no Religious Education taught in schools. There are private religious schools, where children learn about their own faith, but nothing like Religious Education in the UK, where pupils learn about the different religions.

What should you know about religion by the time you leave school? There have been a number of answers to this question. Many people agree that you should be able to identify the main beliefs and practices of the different religions. You should also know about the important people and places in a religion.

However, Religious Education is not just about gathering information. It is also about learning important skills. For example, a course in RE will help you to use religious words and religious language correctly. It will also help you to interpret religious symbols and rituals (**A**).

If you have done a course in RE you should be able to identify the different groups or denominations

A *We need skills to interpret religious symbols and rituals*

in a religion. Studying the history of the world's religions will help you to see the connections and historical links between different faith communities (**B**).

Religious Education can also help you to develop the ability to see another point of view, and to understand what it means to be a member of a faith community. It will show you how a religious belief works in the life of a person and in the life of a community. You will also be able to identify the moral values

B *Some connections and links between the different faith communities*

which guide the lives of religious people. These are often values which religions have given to society as a whole.

Discussion question

Many religious values are at work in society at large and many organizations are based on religious values. What examples of these can you suggest?

Once you have studied a number of religions, you should be able to recognize how religions differ from one another. Sometimes the beliefs and practices of the various religions are expressed in similar ways. For example, many of them communicate through symbols, stories and festivals. However, when we look closer we see there are important differences.

You may want to ask: Do religions really have anything to say to us and how we live our lives? Looking at the answers the different religions offer to the difficult questions in life makes us think about our own beliefs. It can help us sort out our own ideas, values and commitments.

C *Many organizations were founded on religious values*

THINGS TO DO

1 Collect examples of religions and religious people in the news from magazines and newspapers. Fix them into your book. Write a few sentences explaining how RE can help young people understand the world they live in.

2 What religious symbols do you know of? Can you say what they represent? Design a title page for your RE work using different religious symbols. Under each one write the religion it stands for. If you can, explain the meaning of each.

3 Imagine you are in charge of education in a country other than the UK and you are wanting to introduce RE in all state schools. Design a poster or a leaflet to explain what the subject is about and why it is important that it is taught in schools.

4 Look at Diagram **B** which shows the way in which some of the major religions are connected. Write six questions based on the information given there. Exchange your questions with a partner. Give your answers in full sentences.

Hinduism: roots and origins

Not all **Hindus** call their religion Hinduism. Many prefer the term Sanatan **Dharma**. Sanatan means eternal. Dharma means law or religion or duty. The word Hinduism comes from the name of the river Indus, which runs through the north-west of the Indian subcontinent, a fertile area rich in grain. Some say that the story of Hinduism begins in the Indus Valley.

About 4000 years ago the Indus Valley was the home of a great civilization. Archaeology has uncovered the remains of two cities at Mohenjo Daro and Harappa. There are signs that a wealthy and cultured people once lived there. It seems the rulers were priests. Fragments of pottery figures suggest they worshipped a mother goddess (**B**) who ensured the fertility of the land.

There are different views about what happened to the Indus Valley civilization. Some scholars believe that from about 1800 BCE, nomadic (wandering) groups from the north, called Aryans, began to arrive and settle in the area. They brought with them their cattle, their religion and their way of life. The Aryan rulers were warriors. They worshipped Indra the storm god (**C**), and Agni the god of fire and the sun god Savitri.

According to this view, Hinduism grew out of the meeting of two cultures – the Indus Valley civilization and the culture of the Aryans. Therefore, from its earliest beginnings, Hinduism included a wide variety of beliefs and practices.

B *The fertility goddess from the Indus Valley*

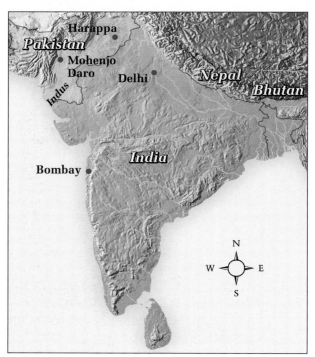

A *The Indian subcontinent*

C *Indra, the storm god*

Discussion question

It is important for people to know where their roots are. For example, many people try to draw up their family tree. Why do you think people need to know where they come from?

Although Hinduism has its roots in India, there are Hindus in many parts of the world. In fact Hinduism is one of the main religions in the UK today. After the Second World War, Britain was short of workers and people from British Commonwealth countries were encouraged to move and take up work there. Many Hindus made their homes in the UK, bringing with them their religion and their way of life. Every religion has to be able to adapt to new circumstances if it is to survive. Hinduism has adapted to meet the needs of its followers in the UK. It has flourished and has enriched the religious life of the country.

D *Hindus at a **shrine** in India*

THINGS TO DO

1 Draw a map of the Indian subcontinent. Add the river Indus, Harappa and Mohenjo Daro. Write two sentences under your map to explain why this area is important if you want to find out about Hinduism.
2 Draw a diagram to show the origins of Hinduism. On one side of the page use words and pictures to represent the Indus Valley civilization and religion. On the other side of the page use words and/or pictures showing aspects of the Aryan culture. Explain your diagram and give it a title.
3 Look at Photos **D** and **E**. Describe what you can see happening in each. Say what is different and what is the same. Why do you think there are such differences between these two examples of Hindu worship?
4 Hindus in the UK trace their family roots back to India. These roots influence their religion, what they eat and their family life. What roots are important to you? Write your answer or draw a map or diagram to illustrate the influences that make you what you are today.

E *Hindu worshipping at a shrine in the UK*

3 Time and creation

Discussion question

How did the world begin? What is the meaning of life? These are deep and difficult questions. What are some of the other great mysteries of life?

Hindus believe there are times when the universe and the world come into being, and other times when everything is destroyed. These are called the days and nights of **Brahma**. Brahma is the god of creation.

According to Hindu tradition, time runs in cycles. In each cycle there are four ages. The first is an age of righteousness, goodness and truth. In each age righteousness declines. The last age is the kali yuga, or dark age, when righteousness is struggling against the powers of evil. At the end of the dark age everything is dissolved.

There are several creation stories in Hindu tradition. Here are three of them:

• Before this time began, this world was darkness. It was unknowable, without form and beyond understanding. It was as if all were in a sleep. Then there was only the one eternal self-existent Being. This Being scattered the darkness and appeared spontaneously. Through the power of thought he created the waters. In these waters he put his seed which became a golden egg as bright as the sun. In this he himself was born – Brahma the father of all worlds. Brahma remained in the egg for a whole year. Then by his own thought, he divided the egg into two and made the heavens and the earth.

A *Vishnu on the waters with Brahma appearing from the lotus flower*

Another creation story begins with a deep fathomless ocean:

- Asleep on the waters, resting in the coils of a giant serpent lay Lord **Vishnu**. From the depths of the ocean came a sound, **Aum**. It grew louder and louder. Vishnu awoke. From his navel grew a lotus flower. In the centre of this golden lotus sat Brahma the Creator (**A**).

  Lord Vishnu commanded Brahma to create the world. Brahma split the lotus flower into three and created the heavens, the skies and the earth below. He created hills and trees, birds and beasts, and filled the world with all kinds of life.

This third story is in the Hindu scriptures called the **Vedas**:

- The breath of life gave birth to the whole world. It breathed its power into all living things. It takes on living creatures like clothes to wear. Therefore all life is one and all depend on the breath of life.

B *The sacred symbol Aum*

1 The seasons of the year and the phases of the moon are examples of cycles. Think of six other examples of cycles in nature or life. What can we learn from these patterns? Can they help us to understand life? Write a poem or words for a song about the cycles or seasons of time and life.

2 Hindus believe that the world is God's creation. Tell one of the stories of creation in words and pictures as if you are preparing a book for young Hindu children. Add a few words at the end to say what you think is the message of this story.

3 The sacred symbol Aum (**B**) represents the infinite, the eternal. Aum is a sound as well as a symbol. Draw the symbol. Say it slowly and think about the sound. Describe in your own words the part Aum plays in the story of creation.

4 Explain the Hindu belief in the breath of life. What does this say about the relationship between humans and animals? Is this different from the way people who are not Hindus might view this relationship? Do you think it would influence the way Hindus treat animals? Think about these questions. Answer them in the form of a discussion between a Hindu and a non-Hindu who is asking the questions.

Beliefs, images and symbols

Is there a God? What is God like? These are questions that have been around for a long time. Hindus believe there is one supreme spirit of the universe. This universal power or spirit they call **Brahman**. Many Hindus translate the word Brahman as God.

Hindus believe that Brahman is not visible to the ordinary eye. But Brahman is everywhere and in everything. Hindus believe that it is possible to see the power of Brahman in the world. For example, you can see God's power to create in the new life of spring. And God's goodness is visible in the lives of those who struggle against evil and who bring righteousness into the world. So God's power is at work in creation and can take on different forms.

Discussion question

How does the Hindu idea of Brahman compare with some of the beliefs about God that you are familiar with?

In Hindu worship the different forms and aspects of God are represented in symbols and images. Ganesha, the elephant-headed god (**A**) symbolizes the power to overcome problems and obstacles. Hindus turn to him to ask for help in conquering hatred, anger and envy which can all prevent true worship and devotion.

The mother goddess (**B**) is an important symbol for Hindus. She has different names and appears in various forms – such as

A *Ganesha, the remover of obstacles*

B *The goddess Durga, her raised hand offers reassurance to the worshipper*

Durga, Kali and Parvati. For many Hindus she represents God's power to protect them from evil.

Symbols are important in all religions. They communicate ideas at a deep level. They work with our feelings as well as our thinking. For example, the pipal tree is often a symbol of holiness in India. Its beauty inspires worship and devotion. The tree represents life and the link between heaven and earth.

The sacred images and symbols used in Hindu worship communicate important truths and teachings about God. Some of them echo stories from the scriptures. For example, the image of Durga shows her carrying weapons. These remind believers of the story in which the goddess overcomes the powers of evil and saves the world.

The images used in Hindu worship are called **murtis**. For many Hindus the murti communicates God's presence in a personal way. Many people keep a picture of someone they love. A photo can bring to life deep feelings or memories of a loved one. In the same way the murti brings to life the presence of God and inspires love and devotion.

THINGS TO DO

1 Write 'What is Brahman?' in a speech bubble from the mouth of a person and draw additional characters to give answers. Do the same with the question 'Why is Brahman hard to represent in a picture or image?' Write a question about the images and symbols of Hinduism and provide answers in the same way. Give your work a title.

2 Look at Photos **A** and **B**. Find the following which are represented in the symbols:
   • strength
   • beauty
   • the power to fight evil
   • the power to reassure those who are afraid
   • the power to remove obstacles.
   Draw symbols to represent these powers, or draw one of the Hindu images and label the symbols, explaining what they stand for.

3 What images or pictures are important in your life? Do you have posters on your wall or photos you treasure? Describe or draw the pictures that mean something to you. Explain why they are important and what they represent.

4 A tree is a powerful symbol in many religions. What does a tree symbolize to you? Is there a particular tree you like or notice? What is special about it? Imagine we had a special day or festival dedicated to trees. How could we celebrate it? Discuss your answers in class. Design a card that you might send. On the back explain the festival and your picture.

5 Symbolic actions and meaning

Symbols communicate meaning and they can be words or pictures. Symbolic actions such as sending flowers, shaking hands, giving a round of applause, also communicate meaning. We know what they represent. However, they could seem strange to anyone from a different culture where these gestures are not normal practice.

Symbolic actions play an important part in Hindu worship. Hindus call worship **puja**. This is performed at a shrine. This is a special place which usually contains an image of a god or goddess. Performing puja is an expression of devotion and love. Puja often includes a number of symbolic actions which help the worshipper to focus their thoughts on God. For example, a bell is rung before the worshipper approaches the image. The image is washed. Offerings of flowers, light, incense and food are put before it as if the god or goddess were a much loved and honoured guest. All the senses are represented in these actions. The worshippers are offering not just words but themselves.

'From the unreal, lead me to the real. From darkness lead me to light. From death lead me to immortality.'
(Brihadaranyaka Upanishad I.iii)

This is a prayer from the Hindu scriptures called the **Upanishads**. Light is an important symbol in Hinduism. It can stand for the presence of God, and represent the light and power of the sun. It can be a symbol of enlightenment – the light of wisdom and truth. Light can also be a sign of life and hope.

Discussion question

If you were lost and in the dark, looking for help and you saw the light of a house in the distance what would it represent for you? What else does light symbolize to you?

There is a Hindu ceremony which welcomes the presence of God. It is called **arti** and involves the offering of light at the shrine. Arti can be performed in the temple or at home. First, the sacred image is washed and offerings of coloured powders, flowers, incense, food and water are given. Then the worshipper lights a small ghee lamp, which is made with clarified butter and five wicks. The lamp is raised up and moved reverently in front of the image, drawing a circle of light in the air before the face of the image (**A**).

A *A Hindu priest turning towards the images to perform arti*

12

B *Worshippers at the temple receiving the arti lamp*

When arti is performed at the temple, the lamp is taken round to the worshippers. They pass their hands over the flame and then over the face and hair (**B**). In this way they receive God's **blessing**.

THINGS TO DO

1 What symbolic actions are part of our everyday life? Using cuttings from magazines and newspapers, make a page of words and pictures illustrating the importance of symbolic actions. Explain their meaning in writing.

2 Describe what is happening in Photos **A** and **B** and explain the meaning of the symbols and symbolic actions.

3 The symbolism of darkness and light is important in religious belief and practice. In a poem or a picture express the feelings and thoughts that come to mind when you experience, think about or imagine darkness and then light.

4 If you were to represent the five senses in a gift to someone you loved, what objects would you choose as symbols? Draw your symbols and explain your choices carefully or write a love poem which includes these symbols and their meaning.

6 The question of evil in Hinduism

One of the hardest questions to answer is: Why is there so much evil in the world? Myths and stories from different religions remind followers that evil must be seen as part of the larger picture of life. It cannot be viewed on its own.

Hindus believe that ignorance was the first evil to come about. According to Hindu tradition, it is often the cause of suffering. One story tells how other evils came into the world. When Brahma had completed creation, he became very hungry. He had made the earth, the hills and the trees. He had made all living things. After this hard work he grew ravenous. Out of the pangs of his hunger hurtled a plague of demons which attacked him and made him angry. From his anger came all manner of evils. These wicked spirits set to work, bringing about all the evil in the world (**A**).

Discussion question

Is ignorance responsible for much suffering in the world today? What examples can you give?

To Hindus there is an answer to the question of suffering and that is the law of **karma**. Karma means actions or the effects of actions. Hindus believe that everything we do has an effect. If we do good, we build up good karma and we will be rewarded with good experiences. If our actions are selfish, unkind or evil, we build up bad karma and we will suffer for it.

After death the soul lives on to be born again in another body and karma from the previous life is carried over. If we have good karma, we will be reborn into a good life.

A *Out of Brahma's anger came all manner of evils*

B *The young Krishna overcoming Kaliya the serpent who poisoned the waters*

If we have bad karma we will pass into a life of suffering. In this way we bring our suffering on ourselves.

Some of the suffering and evil in the world is beyond human control. According to the Hindu scriptures, when the forces of evil become too powerful, God comes to earth to restore righteousness. It is Lord Vishnu who takes on this role. Hindus believe that Vishnu has come to earth in many forms. He came as **Rama** to destroy the ten-headed evil demon, Ravana. Another time he came as Lord **Krishna** to overthrow the evil tyrant, Kamsa. Krishna said:

'For the protection of the good,
For the destruction of evil-doers
For the setting up of righteousness
I come into being age after age.'
(Bhagavad Gita IV, 8)

Many Hindus worship God as Lord Krishna. His birthday is celebrated at the festival of Janmashtami. Worshippers gather at the temple to make offerings at the shrine of Krishna and to remember stories about his birth and childhood. They tell of how the tyrant Kamsa sent spies and demons to destroy the boy. However, each time Krishna is able to bring good out of evil and to save those who are close to him from harm (**B**).

THINGS TO DO

1 Write your own myth of how evil came into the world. Show how it is a part of the process of life.

2 Do you think that there is some truth in the belief that evil comes back to us? Are there times when we suffer because of our wrong-doing? What examples can you think of? Write a discussion between a Hindu and a non-Hindu on the connection between evil and suffering.

3 In Hindu myths and stories evil rears its head in many different forms. What are the different forms of evil in the world today? Design a poster to illustrate your answer to this question.

4 As in other religions, Hinduism teaches that overcoming evil is part of our purpose in life. Many people are not members of a religion so how can this important message be taught to children and young people today? Write your answer in the form of a magazine article for young people.

Shiva

In some Hindu traditions God is seen as having three faces. These are the three aspects represented in Brahma, Vishnu and **Shiva**. Brahma is God the Creator. Vishnu is God the Preserver who is able to come to earth in different forms in order to save it from the powers of evil. Shiva is the Lord of Destruction.

One image of Shiva shows him dancing in a circle of flames (**A**). The circle represents the never-ending cycle of life, death and rebirth. The flames symbolize the power this god has to destroy all things. The heartbeat of the universe is in his hands – he holds a small drum to keep the rhythm. Shiva tramples on a dwarf which represents small-mindedness and ignorance. Shiva represents the eternal search for truth.

Discussion question

When Hindus worship Shiva they are reminded that death is a part of life. They learn to respect the place of death in the pattern of things and accept it. Do people think about death in this way in western society? Do people come to terms with it, or do they try to avoid the reality of death?

Shiva not only has the power to destroy all life, but he is also able to make new. Sometimes Shiva is represented in a smooth rounded pillar of stone (**B**). This symbolizes his power to recreate life. He has control over life and death. Hindus believe that Shiva knows the hour of their death. He also knows what their lives will be in their next existence.

Perhaps the most well known image of Shiva is of him seated in a yoga position in the forests of the Himalayas. Shiva generates

A *Shiva the Lord of Destruction*

B *A Hindu worshipping Lord Shiva*

his mighty powers through long periods of **meditation**, sitting quietly in deep thought. In the centre of his forehead is his third eye. According to Hindu tradition, if this eye were to close the entire universe would be thrown into complete darkness. From his tangled tresses of hair flows the river Ganges. The story is that when the waters of the Ganges first fell to earth, the force was too great. Shiva volunteered to let the waters first break on his head so that they would not destroy the earth. In this way Shiva shows that he is able to prevent destruction as well as bring it about.

Many Hindus worship God as Lord Shiva. Some keep a night of fasting called Shivaratri which usually falls in February. During the fast, worshippers gather at the temple to make offerings at the shrine and to sing hymns of praise.

THINGS TO DO

1 Design an invitation to the temple to keep the night of fasting. Inside your card, write a few sentences to explain the powers of Lord Shiva and to invite worshippers to sing his praises.

2 Draw Shiva dancing and show clearly the different symbols in the image. Explain the meaning of the image in writing.

3 Using examples from your own experience or from the world around you, explain the idea that sometimes new beginnings and new life can spring from the destruction of the old.

4 When Hindus worship Shiva they learn to recognize that death is a part of the cycle of life. Write a scene from a play in which a Hindu talks to a non-Hindu about their views of life and death.

Pilgrimage in Hinduism

A **pilgrimage** is a religious journey. Hindus have different reasons for making a pilgrimage. A particular shrine or temple may be the focus. The worshipper might be fulfilling a vow. For example, a couple wanting a child might make a vow to Durga to undertake a pilgrimage once their prayers have been granted. They will then visit a holy site dedicated to the goddess. Sometimes a pilgrimage is a preparation for death.

Discussion question

Journeys can be times of change and learning. What journeys have you been on where you have learnt a lot?

Whatever the reason for the journey, Hindu pilgrimage is an important act of devotion to God. The change of routine and change of scene provides an opportunity for making other changes. For example, the pilgrim might alter their outlook on life or become more deeply involved in their religion. Hindus believe that pilgrimage helps to build positive karma and to ensure a better existence in the next life. Pilgrimage is often a time of self-discipline and self-sacrifice. People travel with few possessions and give up the comforts of home. Many Hindus in the UK save up for years to get the fare to travel to India on pilgrimage.

There are many holy sites and places of pilgrimage in India. Some are places of great natural beauty. In the Himalayan mountains there are many pilgrimage sites, including the source of the holy river Ganges (**A**).

Every Hindu wants to travel to **Varanasi** at some point in their life. Here, on the banks of

A *Hindu pilgrims in the Himalayas*

B *Pilgrims at Varanasi on the banks of the river Ganges*

the Ganges, pilgrims gather to meditate, bathe, perform puja and to carry out important religious ceremonies (**B**). It is believed that the waters of the Ganges are so sacred they can wash away past karma. Many Hindus travel to Varanasi late in life to wash in the Ganges as a preparation for death. Some pilgrims take the water home to their elderly relatives who cannot travel themselves.

The focus of a pilgrimage can be a person rather than a place. Many Hindus go to hear the teachings of a famous **guru** or religious teacher. They may stay in a religious community in order to spend time in meditation or learning yoga.

In the past Hindus in the UK had to travel to India to carry out acts of pilgrimage. Today many go instead to a religious site in the UK. Krishna's shrine at Bhaktivedanta Manor has become an important place of Hindu pilgrimage. The Swami Narayan temple in Neasden is now also a sacred place for Hindus in the UK.

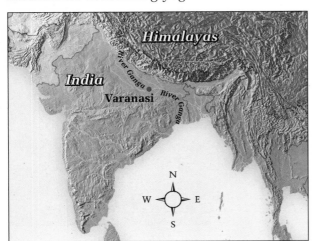

C *The Indian subcontinent*

THINGS TO DO

1 Draw a map of the Indian subcontinent in the centre of a page, allowing plenty of space around it. Mark on it two places of pilgrimage. Use insets to illustrate the sites and explain the importance of these places.
2 A change in routine, new people and new places are all part of the process of pilgrimage. Write a poem about a journey of change that you have made, or an imaginary one.
3 Write an article for a travel brochure describing and explaining Hindu pilgrimage.
4 If you were to make a pilgrimage, where would you go and why? You might choose a place that is very beautiful, or a place of historical or religious importance, or the birthplace of someone famous. Write your answer in the form of a letter to a Hindu friend, explaining how your pilgrimage would be similar or different from a Hindu pilgrimage.

Judaism: the Covenant

Judaism is an ancient religion. It goes back to the leader and **prophet** called **Abraham.** He probably lived about 2000 BCE. He is sometimes called the father of the people of **Israel**.

Jews believe God wanted to talk to people. He wanted them to know and love him. He was looking for someone who would listen. Abraham wanted to know God. God spoke to him and made an agreement with him. Abraham, for his part, was to obey God in all things. He showed he was willing to do this when God asked him to **sacrifice** his son, Isaac. Abraham travelled to the place God commanded and he prepared to kill Isaac. At that moment God stopped him and gave him a ram to sacrifice instead. Abraham had shown he would do anything for God. In return, God promised to make Abraham the father of a great people. They would have a land to live in: the land of **Canaan**. This promise between God and Abraham was called the **Covenant**.

Abraham had a son called Isaac. He, in turn, had a son called Jacob. Jacob's name was changed to Israel. Israel had twelve sons whose families grew into the twelve tribes of Israel (**A**).

Discussion question

Many people are interested in the history of their own families. Why do you think this might be so? How much do you know about the history of your family?

A *Four of the windows in the Hadassah Medical Centre in Jerusalem depicting the twelve tribes of Israel*

B *A Torah scroll*

By the time Abraham's family had become a nation it needed a new Covenant. The people had lived as slaves in Egypt and been led to freedom by **Moses**. He led them through the desert to begin their journey to Canaan, the **Promised Land**. Jews believe God spoke with Moses on Mount Sinai (see page 28) and gave the people of Israel guidelines to help them keep their part of the Covenant and live in partnership with him.

God **revealed** his promises and commandments to Moses on Mount Sinai. Jews call these writings the **Torah**. The Torah was a precious gift (**B**). It was a sign of the special agreement between God and Israel. Like a wedding ring, it was and still is a symbol of a promise of love and faithfulness. It reminded the people that they should not have anything to do with false worship, evil, murder, greed, theft, envy, dishonesty or gossip. They should love God and keep his commands. In return, God promised that they would live in their own land (which later became known as Israel). He would protect and care for them.

The first Jewish communities in Britain arrived soon after the Norman Conquest in the eleventh century. However, they were persecuted and eventually expelled. In 1655 CE they were once again allowed to settle in Britain. At the end of the nineteenth century their numbers grew as Jews fled from persecution in eastern Europe (**C**). Many Jews in Britain today arrived in the 1930s and afterwards in order to escape from the Nazis.

THINGS TO DO

1 Sacrifice always means giving up something which is difficult. What things other than possessions might a person sacrifice? Why do people make sacrifices? In what sorts of circumstances?

2 Perhaps the most well known guidelines given in the Torah are the **Ten Sayings** or Ten Commandments:
   • Worship no god but me
   • Do not make images of anything to worship because I am the Lord your God
   • Do not use God's name for evil purposes
   • Keep the Sabbath day holy
   • Respect your father and your mother
   • Do not commit murder
   • Do not commit adultery
   • Do not steal
   • Do not accuse anyone falsely
   • Do not desire what belongs to others.
   In what ways do you think these are helpful guidelines for today? Are there any you would change and why?

3 During our lives we commit ourselves to all sorts of agreements. Some are more challenging than others. Make a poster to illustrate the sorts of agreements that people enter into. Make it clear what these involve for people on both sides.

4 Find out where the nearest synagogue is and a little about its history. For example:
   • when it was built
   • why it was built in the area it is
   • what type of Jewish community meets there
   • how many members it has
   • whether its membership is increasing or decreasing
   • whether any famous Jews have prayed there.

C *A nineteenth-century synagogue (now a museum) in Manchester*

Symbols in Judaism

Jews believe in one God who made the Covenant with Abraham. The Covenant is kept today by Jews who still obey God's commandments. There are many symbols in Judaism to remind them of this agreement.

On the doorpost of a Jewish home you will find a **mezuzah** (**A**). This is a scroll of parchment. It is often kept in a small cover or container. On the parchment is a section of the Torah which is handwritten in Hebrew. The verses begin the important Jewish prayer called the **Shema**: 'Hear O Israel, the Lord our God is One...'. Jews will often touch the mezuzah as they pass through the door. This reminds them of God's love for them.

Discussion question

Do you think there is anything you should think about or remind yourself of every day? Why?

A *A mezuzah on a doorpost in a Jewish home*

B *Jewish men wear the tefillin and tallit as a sign of the Covenant with God*

Prayers are said every day. On weekdays many Jewish men will wear **tefillin** (**B**). These are two small leather boxes. Inside are pieces of parchment on which are written passages from the Torah. One box is strapped on the forehead. The other is tied to the weaker (usually left) arm.

The mezuzah and tefillin are both signs of the Covenant with God. The Torah says:

'Never forget these commands that I am giving you today… Tie them on your arms and wear them on your foreheads as a reminder. Write them on the doorposts of your houses.'

(Deuteronomy 6:6–9)

Many Jewish men also wear a **tallit** (B) to keep a commandment in the Torah:

'Make tassels on the corners of your garments… The tassels will serve as reminders, and each time you see them you will remember all my commands and obey them; then you will not turn away from me and follow your own wishes and desires. The tassels will remind you to keep all my commands, and you will belong completely to me.'

(Numbers 15:37–40)

Some Jewish men wear an undervest with tassels on. This is called a **tzizit** (C).

C *Jewish boys wearing tzizit to remind them to keep God's commands*

Keeping the food laws found in the Torah is another sign of keeping the Covenant. Jews may only eat foods which are 'fit' or **kosher**. For example, fish have to be those with both fins and scales and meat must only come from animals with parted hooves and which chew the cud. All meat must have had the blood drained from it. The Jewish community has special ways of killing animals and therefore has its own butchers to deal with meat in the correct ways.

Meat and milk products must not be eaten in the same meal. In some homes the two are kept entirely separately. Different cutlery, plates and pots will be used for meat and milk. Some homes even have two sinks, one to wash up after meat foods and one after milk.

By keeping these commandments, Jews are reminded of God throughout every day.

THINGS TO DO

1 The laws of the Covenant are important for the individual and the community. How does keeping certain laws and customs bind people together? Which habits, rules, customs and symbols bind your school together as a community? Discuss this in class.

2 Some Jews think that there are laws and practices which are no longer relevant or meaningful. Some keep a strict kosher kitchen, others do not. What are the dangers of giving up certain traditions of a religion? What are the arguments for change? Discuss these questions in class.

3 Plan meals for a Jewish family for one day. Remember what meats and fish may be eaten. Remember also that meat and milk must not be used in the same meal.

4 Jewish parents must teach the commandments to their children. Read more about the religious laws concerning food in Leviticus 11. Make a poster to illustrate kosher laws, which a Jewish parent could put up in the kitchen for children to see.

11 Creation

Jews believe God has created and cares for everything. The story of how the world was created is found at the beginning of the Torah in the Book of Genesis.

In the beginning there was nothing. God said, 'Let there be light' and he made night and day. The evening came and the morning followed.

A & B *God created night and day*

On the second day God separated the water into the oceans below and the rains above.

Land came from the seas on the third day and God said, 'Let all sorts of plants grow on the earth and produce seeds and fruit.'

On the fourth day God made a powerful light to rule the day and a fainter one to rule the night.

The creatures of the oceans and the air were made on the fifth day.

God made all the animals of the earth on the sixth day.

Then he said, 'Let me make a human. Someone like me, to rule over the other creatures.' So he created man and woman.

Discussion question

Jews and Christians believe human beings were made in the image of God. In what ways do you think they might be thought to be like God?

He blessed them and said, 'Have children and build families. Fill the earth. Be responsible for all the animals. Plough the land and harvest the grain. Enjoy the fruits of the earth.' God was pleased with his creation.

Then he rested. He blessed the seventh day and made it holy.

Some people believe this story is literally true and others do not. However, most agree that it has meaning for people today. It shows a belief in the power of God and his care for the world. Some say that the word 'day' may mean something longer than 24 hours. In this way the story could show the development of the world over time. It suggests human beings are God's most important creation. They have the job of caring for everything else (**C**).

C *God made all the animals on the sixth day and humans to rule over them: lion skins for sale in a trophy shop*

D *Trees are planted during Tu B'Shevat celebrations*

Thanks are given for God's creation in the harvest festivals of **Sukkot** and **Shavuot** (see pages 28–9). Jews also celebrate Tu B'Shevat (New Year for Trees) by planting trees (**D**). They also collect money to pay for them to be planted in other countries. Jews believe this is one way of looking after the world God created.

THINGS TO DO

1 People understand the story of creation in different ways. Some say it is literally true. Others say each day in the story stands for millions of years so the general order of creation in the story is correct. To some its importance is as a story with a meaning – that God created the world; that he allowed people to enjoy it but they also had to care for it. Work in groups. One of you can be an interviewer. The others should each take a point of view. Prepare a programme for radio or television to discuss the different views on the story of Genesis.

2 The story of the creation shows how God gave humankind power over nature but also a responsibility to care for it. Make a poster to illustrate ways in which members of your class could play a part in caring for the environment.

3 Jews believe God gave human beings the responsibility of caring for animals and the environment. They also have the power to rule over them. Some people would say this power has been misused (**C**). Collect information which shows examples of:
   • people's misuse of their power over the environment and the creatures on the earth
   • people's sense of responsibility for the environment.
   Discuss these issues in your class.

4 Jews keep the seventh day of every week as a day of rest as God did in the story. It is called **Shabbat**. Do you think that one day of each week should be set apart from the other six? In what way should it be different? Explain your answer in a short paragraph giving reasons for your point of view. Discuss the different views in the class.

12 Rosh Hashanah and Yom Kippur

Rosh Hashanah (New Year) and **Yom Kippur** (the Day of Atonement) are the most important holy days of the Jewish year. They occur in the early autumn. It is a time of new beginnings.

People can only start afresh after they have thought about changes they want to make in their lives. Rosh Hashanah is the start of ten days when Jews think about the past year. They ask for God's forgiveness. They also ask for forgiveness from people they have hurt or upset. In return, each person has a duty to forgive those who ask them to do so.

Discussion question

It is not always easy to forgive other people. What sorts of things would you find most difficult to forgive and why?

Rosh Hashanah is a time for serious thought and also for hope. People make an effort to put right past mistakes. They wear new clothes and eat fruits which are only just in season. Pieces of apple are dipped in honey to show the hope that the new year will be a sweet one (**A**).

In **synagogues** the **shofar**, or ram's horn, is blown (**B**). One hundred notes will be sounded during the services of Rosh Hashanah. It startles people and reminds them to repent (to be sorry for their wrong-doings).

A *Apples are dipped in honey to show hope for the new year ahead*

B *The shofar being blown at Rosh Hashanah*

The Day of Atonement, Yom Kippur, is ten days after Rosh Hashanah. Atone means 'at one'. To live 'at one' with God is to ask forgiveness for sins and to obey God's commandments. Jews are reminded of Abraham's obedience. The story of his willingness to sacrifice his son is read from the Torah (see page 20).

Yom Kippur is a day of fasting. Jews do not eat or drink for 25 hours beginning at sunset. The synagogue is fuller than usual. There are several services during the day. Some men wear white garments called kittels. Many people stay all day to pray and hear readings from the Torah.

In the afternoon, the book of Jonah is read. It explains how God wanted Jonah to tell the people of Nineveh to repent. Jonah did not want to do so. At last he gave them God's message. They were truly sorry for their sins and fasted and prayed for forgiveness. The story shows God will forgive anyone who is really sorry (see box).

Jews believe Yom Kippur is the day when God decides whether a person's name should remain in the book of life or whether they should die. The day ends with one note from the shofar. It reminds Jews to keep the Covenant and live 'at one' with God.

Jonah

God told Jonah to go to the city of Nineveh. People there were behaving badly. Jonah was to tell them God was angry. Jonah did not want to do this so he got on a ship going in the opposite direction. Soon a storm blew up. All the sailors prayed. They woke Jonah up. He told them he was running away from God and the storm was a punishment for this. He told the sailors to throw him overboard. They did not want to but gave in in the end. The storm stopped. A big fish swallowed Jonah. He stayed inside it for three days, praying. Then the fish spewed him on to a beach.

Once again God told Jonah to go to Nineveh. This time he went. He told the people that God would destroy the city in forty days because of their wickedness. The people took the warning seriously. As a sign of how sorry they were, they all dressed in sackcloth; even the king. They all fasted. God saw that they were truly sorry and so he did not punish them. Jonah was cross that God had changed his mind. God showed him it would have been unfair to punish people who were truly sorry and determined to do better.

THINGS TO DO

1 Many centuries ago at Yom Kippur, there used to be a special service in which a goat would be led out into the desert. People believed it was taking everyone's sins with it. From this custom we get the word 'scapegoat'. The dictionary says a scapegoat is a person who carries the blame for something that is someone else's fault. Try to describe a situation in which we might use the word today.

2 Read the story of Jonah in the box. Many people believe this teaches some important lessons. Answer the following questions:
   - How might Jonah's experience show people they should obey God?
   - What might the story show about God's willingness to forgive people?
   - How might the story show that God can control everything in the world?
   - What do you think about the messages of this story?
   Explain why you think what you do.

3 Rosh Hashanah is a time of judgement when God decides whether people should be punished. What difference do you think believing this might make to the everyday life of a person? Discuss this in groups and write down your thoughts.

4 Starting afresh usually means people have to set their own targets for improvement. Write down the targets you would set yourself for next year and explain why you have chosen them.

God's care for his people

There are three important festivals which remind Jews of their belief that God helped their ancestors to escape from slavery in Egypt.

God is believed to have chosen a man called Moses to lead the Jewish people. He had many meetings with the Pharaoh of Egypt to try to persuade him to set them free from slavery. Only after the last of ten disasters (usually called the ten plagues) did Pharaoh agree, when the eldest son in every Egyptian family had died. Moses had made the people of Israel prepare carefully for the night on which this happened. Lambs were killed and blood wiped on the doorposts of their homes. The homes protected in this way were not visited by God's angel of death. The angel passed over them.

The following morning the slaves were ordered to leave Egypt very quickly. They were not even given time to prepare their bread dough with yeast and cook it. This escape is known as the **Exodus**.

Jews believe God continued to guide the people, with Moses as their leader, as they wandered in the desert. They were homeless and had to build temporary shelters. They relied on God to protect them. At Mount Sinai Jews believe God gave Moses the Torah in order to provide the people with guidelines by which to live. He renewed his Covenant with Israel (see page 20). If the people obeyed his laws he would give them a land to live in and he would make them a great nation.

The festival of **Pesach** (in spring) is a reminder of the Exodus from Egypt.

The festival of Sukkot in the autumn reminds Jews of the time God protected their ancestors while they lived in temporary shelters in the desert. Today

A *A sukkah reminds Jews of their temporary shelters and God's protection*

B *The lulav and etrog are symbols used at Sukkot*

C *The ten commandments (part of the Torah) on tablets of stone in a synagogue*

shelters, or sukkot, are built by Jewish families (**A**). The roof of each sukkah is made of branches and leaves. Gaps are left through which stars can be seen. Meals are eaten in the sukkot and, if the weather allows, Jews may sleep in them.

Jews also remember God's care for the whole world when they wave the lulav and etrog in all directions (**B**). The etrog is a citrus fruit. The lulav is made from branches of palm, willow and myrtle. Some say these things stand for different parts of the body:

- the etrog – the heart
- the palm – the spine
- the willow – the lips
- the myrtle – the eyes.

They remind Jews that they should serve God with their whole being.

Discussion question

What do you think it would mean to serve God with the parts of the body represented by the lulav and etrog?

At the festival of Shavuot, Jews celebrate the giving of God's precious gift, the Torah, to Moses on Mount Sinai (**C**). The book of Ruth is read in the synagogue.

THINGS TO DO

1 When Jews celebrate Pesach, they do not just remember the escape of the Israelite slaves from Egypt as if it were something that happened more than 3000 years ago. Instead each person imagines that he or she was actually one of the slaves who suffered so much and was eventually set free. Imagine you were one of those slaves. Write about your last days in Egypt and your escape.

2 Look back at the text in this unit. Can you discover why the name for Pesach in English is Passover? Explain the reason in your own words.

3 Shavuot and Sukkot are both harvest festivals. They celebrate the gathering in of grain and fruit. Many people today live in towns and some hardly ever see crops growing. A dictionary says the word 'harvest' can also refer to the product of any action, not just the gathering in of grain or other products. Work in a group and discuss what might be meant by the phrases 'industrial harvest' and 'the fruit of our labours'. Plan a harvest celebration which is not linked with food crops but with other products needed, or wanted, by people today.

4 Shavuot and Sukkot encourage Jews to think about things they are thankful for. Discuss some of the big things in your life that you feel thankful for.

Pesach

Pesach lasts for seven or eight days. The most important part of the festival is the **seder**. This service takes place in Jewish homes on the first two nights of Pesach. (In Israel it is only on the first night.) 'Seder' means order. The service includes a symbolic meal and retells the story of the Exodus.

Candles are lit and blessings said over the wine. The youngest child asks, 'Why is this night different from all other nights?' In answering this and other questions the leader of the seder tells the story of the escape from slavery in Egypt. Everyone can follow the story in a book called the **Hagadah**. During the telling, symbolic foods are eaten and wine is drunk (**A**).

A *The symbolic foods of the seder meal*

- Matzah is bread made without yeast – unleavened bread. It reminds Jews of how quickly the slaves had to leave Egypt. They did not have time to let their bread dough rise.
- A shankbone of lamb is placed on the seder plate but not eaten. It represents the lambs killed so that blood could be put on the doorposts of homes to protect them from God's angel of death.
- A roasted egg is a symbol of the sacrifices which used to be made in the temple.
- Maror, or bitter herbs, is lettuce because it has a bitter stalk. Sometimes freshly grated horseradish is used. Maror reminds Jews of how horrible slavery was.
- Haroset, a mixture of apples, nuts, cinnamon and wine, stands for the cement used by the slaves in building work.
- Carpas, a green vegetable, usually parsley, is a sign of spring. This is dipped in salt water to remind people of the slaves' tears.

Wine is used in all celebrations. Some drops may be spilled when the ten plagues are mentioned. This shows that although they brought happiness and freedom to the people of Israel, they brought sadness and suffering to others. A glass is poured for the prophet **Elijah** because it is believed he will return before all the people of the world are free. Someone may open the door to see if he has arrived. This custom took on a new importance in twelfth century Britain when Jews were accused of drinking human blood at Pesach. By opening their doors, Jews showed they had nothing to hide and that the accusation was not true.

Discussion question

Do you think people should have the freedom to follow any religion they choose, no matter where they live? Try to consider different views in your discussion.

B *Candles are lit each night of Hanukkah*

Besides Pesach, there are other festivals that celebrate the escape of Jews from some form of persecution. **Hanukkah**, in winter, recalls the rededication of the temple by the Maccabees after they fought and defeated the Greeks who were ruling Israel at the time. To mark this triumph, candles or oil lamps are lit each night of the eight-day festival (**B**).

The spring festival of **Purim** celebrates the escape of Jews in the Persian Empire from persecution and death. This is a festival of fun and merriment (**C**).

Hanukkah and Purim also remind people of the need to stand firm in their faith.

C *There are often fancy dress parades and parties to celebrate Purim*

THINGS TO DO

1 A local primary school has found out that your class is studying Pesach. You have been invited to talk to one of the classes and set up a display which will explain the seder meal and the festival. In a group, draw up your plans showing how you will do this.

2 Jewish families clean their homes thoroughly before Pesach to ensure that there are no traces of leavened food left. Leaven is anything which will make dough rise like yeast and self-raising flour. In some strict homes pots, pans, plates, cups and cutlery which are normally used with leavened foods are not used during Pesach.
   • Write a plan of how you would set about cleaning your home in preparation for Pesach. Remember especially any places where crumbs of food might be trapped.
   • Draw up a list of all the different cooking and eating equipment you would need to make sure food could be prepared and eaten during Pesach without coming into contact with anything which had touched leavened foods.

3 Light is an important symbol in the celebration of Hanukkah, and food in the Pesach festivities. Think of as many ways as you can in which light and food are used in other celebrations. If possible, find other books on Jewish festivals and celebrations. Choose either light or food and discover as much as you can about how each one features in other Jewish celebrations and customs.

4 The stories of the festivals of Pesach, Hanukkah and Purim all tell of how Jewish people helped to rescue their communities. Moses helped the slaves escape from Egypt. Judas Maccabeus led a group of rebels to capture the temple from foreign rulers and re-dedicate it to God. Queen Esther helped save the Jews living in the Persian Empire from persecution and death. The United Nations Declaration of Human Rights lists many things which people believe all human beings have a right to. It also makes it clear that everyone has duties to the community. Do you agree with this? If you do, what do you think your duties are?

Israel

A *Map showing the position of Israel*

For many generations Jews have lived all over the world. However, most of them still look upon Israel as their spiritual homeland (**A**). It is the land Jews believe was promised to Abraham by God in the Covenant. Many Jews want to visit Israel. It is a chance to refresh their faith and feel in touch with the traditions and history of their people and religion.

There are places of religious and historical interest all over Israel but the most important is the holy city of **Jerusalem**. It was there, in the tenth century BCE, that the first temple was built. Later destroyed and rebuilt, it was for centuries the centre of Jewish worship. It was only in the temple, supervised by priests, that sacrifices could be made. At festival times, especially Sukkot, Pesach and Shavuot, thousands of people would travel to the holy city.

Discussion question

Can you suggest possible advantages and disadvantages of having only one place in which sacrifices could be offered?

The temple was finally destroyed in 70 CE. All that remains today is part of its outer wall. This is known as the Western Wall (**B**). Some aspects of worship in the temple, like sacrifices, no longer exist in Judaism. However, to visit this centre of worship can

B *Worshippers at the Western Wall in Jerusalem*

C *Yad Vashem is a memorial to those who died in the Holocaust*

D *A light is kept burning in the hall of remembrance at Yad Vashem*

be a very moving experience. It reminds people that God is, and always has been, at the centre of Jewish life. It is a focus for all Jews today. It also reminds them of their history and links them with generations of Jews who have worshipped there.

Many Jews go to the Western Wall to pray. Some like to write their prayers on small pieces of paper and put them in between the great stones. The area is always very crowded on Shabbat and at festival times. Just as, in the past, people celebrated festivals in the temple, so today many Jews make a pilgrimage to the Western Wall on some of these special occasions, if they can.

A more modern place which many people visit in Jerusalem is Yad Vashem (**C**). This building and surrounding grounds are a memorial to all the Jews who died in the **Holocaust**. The **Gentiles** who helped them are also remembered here. A light is kept burning in the large hall of remembrance (**D**). On the floor are the names of camps in which Jews were held and killed. Visitors are reminded of the scale of the tragedy: six million Jewish lives were lost. Many are moved to tears.

Jews are united by their belief in the one God and also by their history. The Western Wall and Yad Vashem are two places which remind them of this history.

THINGS TO DO

1 Explain in your own words why so many Jews look upon Israel as their spiritual homeland. Unit 9 on pages 20–21 might help you.

2 The temple in Jerusalem was the centre of Jewish worship for centuries. Jews still worship at what remains of it today. Do you think it is important for people to have definite places where they can worship God or can they do so anywhere? Discuss this in your class and try to make a list of the advantages and disadvantages of having particular places for worship.

3 Some people still try to convince others that the Holocaust did not happen. In March 1997, a leaflet was found in copies of Anne Frank's diary in bookshops in London. It said that the book was a fraud written to convince people of the 'Holocaust legend'. One member of staff was so upset that she burst into tears. Why would this leaflet cause such distress? Why do so many people believe it is important to teach young people about the Holocaust? Why do so many people visit Yad Vashem?

4 Try to explain why the Western Wall and Yad Vashem are important places of pilgrimage for so many Jews.

The spread of Buddhism

The current teaching of Buddhism began in northern India with the life and teachings of Gotama **Buddha** (Buddha means enlightened being). He was born in about 563 BCE. When he grew up he went in search of the truth about life. Having found it, he spent the rest of his life teaching others how they might also find **enlightenment**. His teachings became popular and he had many followers. They came to be known as **Buddhists**.

After his passing away, the Buddha's followers took his message to other parts of India. It gradually spread eastwards to places like Sri Lanka, Myanmar and Thailand in the south, and Nepal, Bhutan, China and Japan in the north (**A**).

One of the people who played an important part in the spread of Buddhism was the Emperor Asoka. In the third century BCE he ruled most of India. He became a Buddhist after feeling very sad and distressed that so many people had been killed in the battles fought to make his empire bigger. He learned from Buddhist teachers. He became well known for his efforts to build a peaceful society. One of the things he did was to send **missionaries** to many places to spread the teachings of the Buddha. His own son and daughter went to Sri Lanka. They brought Buddhism there in 250 BCE. Asoka believed it was important for people to respect each other's religions.

Discussion question

Why do you think Asoka wanted to send missionaries to spread the teachings of the Buddha?

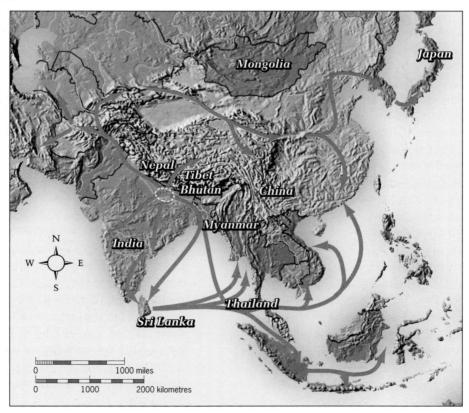

A *After the Buddha's passing away, his followers spread his message far and wide*

B *Monks travelled to Britain to teach about Buddhism*

C *Western Buddhists at Chithurst monastry in the south of England*

As it spread, Buddhism met and was influenced a little by other religions. Different traditions developed in different countries. Gradually three main types of Buddhism could be seen. **Theravada** Buddhism became the main form in Sri Lanka, Myanmar and Thailand. This tradition claims to carry on the earliest beliefs and practices and to have scriptures (the **Pali Canon**) which contain the actual words of Gotama Buddha. The Buddhism found most strongly in China and Japan is known as **Mahayana** Buddhism and that in Tibet and Mongolia is called **Vajrayana** Buddhism. The different forms emphasize different paths to enlightenment.

For centuries very little was known about Buddhism in the West. Travellers and scholars, particularly from America, Germany and Britain, began to learn about it from the early years of the nineteenth century. However, Buddhism was not practised in Britain until early in the twentieth century. In 1926 the Buddhist Society was formed. Monks or Bhikkus from the Far East travelled to Britain to teach about different forms of Buddhism (**B**). After the Chinese invasion of Tibet in 1951, a number of monks escaped to find safety in Britain. Later refugees from Vietnam increased the number of practising Buddhists. However, most Buddhists in Britain are people who have personally chosen to adopt this way of life (**C**).

THINGS TO DO

1 Draw a map to show countries in which Buddhism has been one of the major religions. Indicate in which countries Buddhists follow the Theravada, Mahayana and Vajrayana traditions.

2 Emperor Asoka thought it was important that people should respect one another's religious beliefs. Britain is a country which allows people to practise whatever religion they choose. Young people are required to learn about the world's great religions in Religious Education lessons. Discuss the benefits and difficulties of these ideals.

3 Asoka wanted to develop and encourage a peaceful society. Throughout history this seems to have been an impossible dream. Do you think it is possible to have a peaceful society? If so how do you suggest it might be brought about? Discuss your views and make a list of guidelines for a more peaceful world.

4 Different forms of Buddhism have developed, emphasizing different aspects of its beliefs and practices. For what reasons do some religious groups remain faithful to their origins and others alter according to the times and places they are in?

Gotama Buddha

Buddhism in all its forms has grown from the experience and teaching of Gotama Buddha. He was born a prince in Lumbini in northern India and was called Siddhattha Gotama. His family belonged to the princely caste and followed the ancient Vedic religion of India. His mother had a strange dream before the birth of her son. She dreamt that a white elephant had entered her side. White elephants are extremely rare. She felt this was a sign that the child would be unusual. It is said that the birth was miraculous and caused her no pain at all. A wise man predicted that the boy would be a great and powerful ruler. However, if he were once to see suffering he would become a wise and revered holy man.

Gotama's father did not want his son to become a holy man who would give up everything to live in the forest. So he took good care to see that Gotama never saw or heard of any suffering. Gotama grew up in his father's palaces. He married and had a child of his own. Despite the fact that there was nothing wrong in his life, Gotama was haunted by a feeling of restlessness. One day he persuaded his charioteer to take him out. The things he saw outside the palace were to change his life. He saw an elderly and decrepit person (**A**). He saw a sick person in pain. He saw a dead body on the way to cremation. Then he saw a holy man who had given up all he owned (**B**). This man had a special look about him that other people did not have.

A *Gotama saw old age for the first time*

B *Gotama saw a holy man and gave up all he owned*

Gotama gave up his life in the palace to find the truth for the benefit of others. He left his wife and child and exchanged his fine clothes for the rags of a wandering holy man.

Discussion question

Seeing signs of old age, sickness and death had a strong effect on Gotama. It led him to change his life. Have you ever seen anything, pleasant or upsetting, which has influenced you?

In the hope of overcoming suffering he joined a group of much respected forest-dwelling holy men. They had given up everything to devote their lives to the search for truth. Gotama practised the hardest meditation exercises and **fasted** (went without food) almost to the point of death. However, he felt this was pointless. He broke his fast and ate a small meal of rice. His friends left him in disgust. Gotama seated himself under a sacred **Bodhi tree** (**C**) to meditate. He made up his mind not to move until he realized the truth. Under the Bodhi tree, Gotama gained enlightenment. He realized the truth about life and the path to peace. He was no longer burning with desires of selfishness and fears of suffering and death. He found the peace of **Nibbana**. Nibbana means 'blown out' like a flame. It is often described as a state of bliss or liberation (being freed).

C *The Bodhi tree, also known as the Tree of Wisdom*

THINGS TO DO

1 Gotama was kept away from all signs of suffering. Would it be possible to do this today? It is quite natural for parents to want to shield their young children from the terrible things in the world. Do you think this is a good idea? Would you want your parents to do this for you? Would you do the same for your child? Discuss these questions in class.

2 The birth stories of great religious leaders often tell of signs and miracles. Why do you think this is? What other birth stories do you know? Compare two and discuss the similarities and differences in class.

3 Is it possible to be completely happy knowing that life eventually ends in death? Discuss this question in groups. Share your ideas in class. Make a class survey of responses.

4 Gotama's father did not want him to give up his comfortable life as a prince. How important do you think money and wealth are in making people happy? Make a collage showing things that give you real happiness.

Buddha images

Buddhists revere Gotama Buddha as a special man because he achieved enlightenment. Homes and shrine rooms usually have images of the Buddha. These remind Buddhists of him and his teaching. Offerings of flowers, incense and light are made as a sign of respect.

Images of the Buddha are called **rupas**. They come in several forms. There are three main positions: sitting, standing and lying down. The seated image is probably the most common. Very often Gotama will be shown in a full or half **lotus position**. He may, however, be seated on a throne. A standing image may depict the Buddha still or walking. When lying down, the image symbolizes the Buddha's entry into Nibbana at the end of his life.

Rupas have several different hand gestures called **muddas**. Each represents an intention or activity. When the hands are across the body on a seated image, with one hand over the other it means meditation (**A**). The fingers of both, or just one hand, making a circle illustrates the Buddha teaching. The right hand turned outwards with fingers pointing down, symbolizes giving. The right hand raised, with the palm turned outwards gives anyone approaching a sense of confidence and protection. It is often seen as a blessing (**B**).

A *Buddha in meditation*

B *Buddha offering protection and blessing*

A seated Buddha touching the ground with his right hand turned inwards is a reminder of the time when Gotama was meditating before his enlightenment (**C**). Mara, the god of temptation and death, tried to destroy his concentration. First he sent his sons Flurry, Hilarity and Pride, but without success. Then it was the turn of his daughters, Discontent, Delight and Thirst. Still Gotama remained unmoved. Nothing could destroy his meditation. He touched the earth for it to witness that he was worthy of enlightenment.

Discussion question

How easy do you find it to concentrate for a long time? What helps you to concentrate and what things distract you?

Other features of Buddha images show Gotama to have been a special person. Long ear lobes remind people that he gave up a royal lifestyle where he would have worn heavy jewellery. There is usually a bump on his head. This is sometimes said to symbolize his wisdom. It may be a reminder of the turban-like headwear he would have worn as a prince. The bump is sometimes small but can also be long and pointed. On some images it appears as a flame-like head-dress. This is a symbol of enlightenment. There is often a halo on the image. This can be a circle or even flame-shaped. On some it is the hood of a snake. This reminds people of the story of how Mucalinda, the snake, protected the Buddha from a storm while he was meditating. He wrapped him in his coils and spread his hood over his head.

Buddha images are always shown the greatest care and respect.

THINGS TO DO

1 Images of the Buddha are often said to fill people with a sense of peace. Look at the pictures in this Unit and try to say how they make you feel.

C *Gotama Buddha meditating before enlightenment*

2 Make an illustrated poster to explain the symbolism of Buddha rupas.

3 Many people believe the story of Gotama's temptation by Mara is not literally true. It is a story with a meaning. It shows that Gotama had to struggle with many inner temptations before he achieved enlightenment. Look at the names of Mara's children. What kind of temptations do you think they show Gotama experienced?

4 Gestures are powerful ways of giving messages. Work in a group to list as many hand gestures as you can think of with their meanings. Discuss the positive and negative messages that can be given. Think of some well known examples of occasions when hand gestures have been used to give messages.

Symbols in Buddhism

For many years after Gotama Buddha's passing away, no images of him were made. Other things became symbols of his life and teaching. These are still used today. The Bodhi tree, under which Gotama sat to meditate, and the lotus flower are symbols of enlightenment. The lotus grows out of deep muddy water and becomes a most beautiful blossom. It is often given as an offering at a shrine. Images of the Buddha are often shown seated on a lotus flower. The wheel is an ancient Indian symbol. It stands for the wheel of law. In Buddhism it is often drawn with eight spokes to symbolize the **Eightfold Path (A)**. This is the guideline for life taught by Gotama Buddha.

There are other symbols which help Buddhists on their way to enlightenment but they have less to do with Gotama Buddha.

A strong belief in **bodhisattvas** became important in Mahayana Buddhism. A bodhisattva is a being who puts off entry into nibbana in order to help others towards enlightenment. Some are seen as spiritual beings who appear in different forms to help others. One of the most well known is **Bodhisattva Avalokiteshvara (B)**. He is a being of unending kindness and compassion. He looks on the world and sees people struggling with life. He wants to help everyone towards happiness. For this reason he has eleven heads and a thousand arms. Each arm has a hand to help others. On each hand there is an eye to help him see the true needs of people. In the hands there are also objects which will enable him

A *The eight-spoked Buddhist wheel representing the Eightfold Path*

B *Bodhisattva Avalokiteshvara is a being of unending kindness*

C *Pu-Tai, or the Laughing Buddha*

to help. Some Mahayana Buddhists worship Bodhisattva Avalokiteshvara. In the Tibetan tradition, people believe the religious leader known as the **Dalai Lama** is a **reincarnation** of this bodhisattva.

Another well known image of Buddhism is often called the Laughing Buddha (**C**). This is not Gotama Buddha but usually understood to be **Pu-Tai**, the Buddha who will come in the future. He looks well fed and happy to show what life will be like when he comes.

Discussion question

After reading the next paragraph, why do you think these aspects of Buddhism are called 'jewels'?

Quite a different symbol stands for the **Three Jewels** of Buddhism (**D**). It is used as a badge by members of a group known as the **Western Buddhist Order** started by an Englishman in the 1960s. The Jewels are the Buddha, the

Dhamma and the **Sangha**. The Buddha's life is an example to follow. The Dhamma is the truth about life. It also means the Buddha's teachings. The Sangha is the community of Buddhist monks and nuns. Sometimes it means all Buddhists. All three are important in helping to inspire and support Buddhists on their path to enlightenment.

D *The Three Jewels*

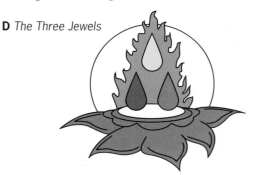

THINGS TO DO

1 If you wanted to help people less fortunate than yourself, what objects would you choose to help you with your task? Explain why.

2 Avalokiteshvara illustrates the ideal of compassion for all beings. Always being kind to others can be quite a challenge. Discuss in a group some of the rewards and difficulties of always being kind and helpful to others.

3 The Sangha, or Buddhist community, can help an individual on the path to greater understanding and enlightenment. In what ways can being part of a religious community help to strengthen the faith of an individual? You might be able to think about other religions you have studied as well to help you answer this question.

4 Do a survey in the class to find out whether people belong to groups which have any kind of rules or guidelines for members. How do they feel about being members of such groups? Do they find keeping the guidelines difficult? Are there any benefits or difficulties arising from membership? Write a report of your findings.

20 Important occasions

Buddhist festivals focus on the life of the Buddha or the life of the Sangha. Traditionally, Buddhist monks travelled from place to place teaching the Dhamma. In India, where Buddhism first grew up, the heavy rains of the monsoon prevented the monks from travelling for three months of the year and they had to take shelter. This became known as the **Rains Retreat**. Originally the local community offered shelter and welcomed their visitors with a great procession. Most monks now stay in their own temple at this time, but the season is still a festive time when **lay** Buddhists (those who are not monks or nuns) visit with gifts of food.

During this time, lay people may also try to pay more attention to their religion. Some stay at the monastery for a while in order to do this. In this way the Sangha and the lay community support one another – the **laity** bring gifts of food while the Sangha gives them spiritual guidance and inspiration. The Sangha sometimes also provides education for boys and young men (sometimes girls as well). In certain parts of the world at this time of year some take part in a ceremony which allows them to live in the temple. For most this will be a time to learn about their religion before they carry on with life in the outside world (**A**).

At the end of the Rains Retreat there is an important occasion called the **Kathina** ceremony. Kathina means cloth or robe. Lay people give the Sangha cloth from which a new robe can be made (**B**). It has to be cut out and made by the monks. The task must be finished within a day. Buddhists gain **merit** (spiritual reward) by giving the cloth.

Discussion question

Why do you think Buddhist monks wear robes like those in the pictures rather than the ordinary clothes of their region?

A *Boys receive education from the Sangha*

B *Lay Buddhists present bhikkhus with cloth at Kathina*

In the Theravada tradition, full moon and new moon and the mid-points between, are times when bhikkhus (monks) and bhikkhunis (nuns) have to think about their failures and speak about their moments of weakness or unkindness. These are called **Uposatha** days. Most people do not go to work on Uposatha days and they make a point of not eating any meat. Families get together to provide a meal for the Sangha. Some spend the whole day there visiting the shrine and listening to the teachings.

The Western Buddhist Order has three special days which encourage its members to concentrate on the Three Jewels of Buddhism. These are called Buddha Day, Dhamma Day and Sangha Day. On each there is an atmosphere of celebration and also opportunities for meditation. There are talks to listen to. On Buddha Day, people celebrate the enlightenment of the Buddha and remember his wisdom and compassion. Dhamma Day concentrates upon the Buddha's teaching and how this can be spread (**C**). The theme of Sangha Day is friendship and harmony. The Buddha taught that peace and harmony are very important.

THINGS TO DO

1 The rainy season is a time for retreat. How would you spend three months on retreat? Imagine you are out in the country, you have no television or other entertainment

C *Balloons released at Dhamma Day celebrations*

and no money, but you are provided with water, food, a library and shelter. How could you make this a valuable time? Discuss this in class.

2 In what ways do the Sangha and lay people in Buddhism support one another? What do you think is meant by spiritual guidance and inspiration? Work with a partner and try to think of examples of relationships between individuals or groups which show how both support each other.

3 Why do you think Buddhist monks and nuns are encouraged to think regularly about their failures and speak about their moments of weakness or unkindness? In what ways might they benefit? How do you think you would feel if you were asked to do this?

4 Peace and harmony are important in Buddhism. Either design a symbol or create a collage to illustrate these ideas.

21 Festivals of the Buddha

The best known Buddhist festival is **Wesak**. Theravada Buddhists celebrate the birth, enlightenment and passing away of the Buddha together.

Discussion question

Why do you think the passing away of the Buddha is celebrated? (Unit 18 might help you answer this.)

Theravada Buddhists say these three events all happened on the same day of the year. People show their respect for the Buddha and his teachings. They hope to gain merit for a better **rebirth**. Buddhists believe people are reborn time and time again until they achieve enlightenment.

The customs and traditions of Wesak vary. In some communities, lanterns and lamps are lit at dusk around the temples and shrines. Some temples have a Bodhi tree which is a symbol of the enlightenment of the Buddha. At Wesak the tree is watered and decorated with lanterns. The lay community arrives at the monasteries, temples and shrines with gifts of food for the monks and with traditional offerings to put before the Buddha image (**A**). Lights represent the light of understanding that the Buddha's teaching can bring. They also symbolize his enlightenment. Flowers show how fragile and short life is. When he was enlightened, the Buddha came to understand the causes of suffering. He said they are people's greed, hatred and ignorance. He claimed that many people do not fully understand that everything changes and that nothing can stay the same. People's lives come to an end. Not understanding and accepting this causes people to be unhappy.

A *Flowers are offered to show how fragile and short life is*

B *Buddhists listen to talks about the Dhamma*

C *Torchlight procession at the Esala Perahera, with an elephant carrying a copy of the container in which the Buddha's tooth is said to be kept*

People listen to talks about the Dhamma (**B**). In many Buddhist countries at Wesak, talks are broadcast over the television and radio so people can hear them at home. Some lay Buddhists spend this special time fasting or in silence. In this way they remember the passing away of the Buddha as well as his enlightenment. Wesak parties are arranged for children and for adults there are opportunities to practise meditation, to hear the teachings of the Buddha and to join in the life of the Sangha in the temple.

Some festivals have become famous even though they are not widely celebrated. One of these takes place in Kandy, Sri Lanka. Buddhists believe that one of the Buddha's teeth is in the temple there. The **Esala Perahera** takes place in July/August. Every evening for two weeks there are great processions through the streets. On the last night a copy of the container in which the tooth is kept is carried on the back of an elephant. The container with the tooth is too valuable to go out in the street. There is great excitement as people crowd the pavements and shop fronts. The music is loud and it can get very hot with all the torches of flame. The elephants with colourful covers and lights around their bodies look spectacular (**C**). The Buddha's tooth is a treasured **relic** and this festival shows the strong Buddhist history of Sri Lanka.

THINGS TO DO

1. Festivals help to bring the community together and encourage people to remember the religious side to their life. Make a leaflet or poster for a temple in Britain to advertise and explain Wesak and to invite people to join in its celebrations.
2. Some Buddhists spend part of the Wesak festival in silence. Discuss in a group how you feel about being silent. Try to think of several situations which would make you feel differently about it.
3. Why do you think relics, or remains, of the Buddha, like the tooth and other things, such as his hair, believed to be in **stupas**, mean so much to many Buddhists? Try to find out about the keeping and use of relics in other religions.
4. The Esala Perahera is a great tourist attraction. So is the temple in Kandy where Buddhists believe the Buddha's tooth is kept. When local people go there to worship, there are often coachloads of tourists watching what is going on. Discuss in your class some of the advantages and disadvantages of encouraging tourists in such places and at such events. Are there advantages and disadvantages in encouraging people who are not taking part to watch services and ceremonies in places of worship?

22 Pilgrimage

Gotama Buddha recommended that followers of his teachings should visit four places which were important in his life. These were the places of his birth, enlightenment, first sermon and passing away. When Buddhism almost died out in India these sites fell into disrepair. In the nineteenth century they were restored.

Perhaps the most important of these is Bodh Gaya where Gotama sat under the Bodhi tree until he achieved enlightenment (**A**). Some say that all Buddhas have been and will be enlightened at Bodh Gaya. Many Buddhists believe it is a place of spiritual power. This is made stronger by the great numbers of pilgrims who visit each year. Today the Mahabodhi (Great Enlightenment) Temple at Bodh Gaya contains a statue of Gotama Buddha. Nearby is a Bodhi tree. It is a descendant of the one under which Gotama sat. Pilgrims tie prayer flags to the tree and many sit to meditate underneath it. There is also a stone on which there is an image of the Buddha's footprint. This is a symbol of his presence.

Even if pilgrims are unable to go to India, there are important places elsewhere in the world. After his passing away the remains of the Buddha, his ashes and items like some hair, were buried in eight stupas or burial mounds. Later these relics were divided and spread further afield. From the earliest times stupas became places of pilgrimage (**B**).

Discussion question

In many religions it is common to have memorials for the lives of relatives and friends. Why do you think people find this so important?

A *Pilgrims visit Bodh Gaya where Gotama sat under the Bodhi tree until he achieved enlightenment*

B *From earliest times stupas have been places of pilgrimage*

Another popular place to visit is Sri Pada (Honourable Footprint) in Sri Lanka (**C**). This is a mountain which rises very steeply from the beautiful area around it. On top there is a large indentation which is said to be a footprint of Gotama Buddha. Visitors climb a very long, steep set of rocky steps carved out of the mountainside. It is the custom to go up the mountain at night and remain there to see the sun rise.

At places of pilgrimage, Buddhists make offerings of flowers, incense and light. They give gifts to the monks living there. They also meditate or think deeply about life.

Buddhists believe in rebirth. Visiting holy places earns them merit which helps them to achieve a better rebirth. That means one which will bring them closer to enlightenment. It is not actually being in any particular place which does this, however. What makes a pilgrimage special is what it does to the inner life of a person. Many find that being away from their normal lives and mixing with other Buddhists at these special places can help them concentrate on the Buddha's teachings. It can also inspire them to follow more strictly the Buddha's guidelines for life.

C *Pilgrims at Sri Pada in Sri Lanka*

THINGS TO DO

1 Using the photographs and text in this Unit to help you, describe:
   • what pilgrims find at Bodh Gaya
   • the pilgrimage to Sri Pada.
2 Any place connected with the life of the Buddha is of interest to Buddhists. Why did the places of his birth, enlightenment, first sermon and passing away become more important than other places in which he lived and taught?
3 Gotama Buddha achieved enlightenment at Bodh Gaya. Perhaps you have heard people say things like, 'Can you enlighten me?' or 'I've seen the light'. What other similar phrases can you think of? Try to explain what they mean.
4 As well as its connection with Gotama Buddha, Sri Pada is a very beautiful place. To be on the top of the mountain at sunrise can be a most inspiring experience. Have you ever seen something which you thought looked wonderful and stirred up strong feelings inside you? Write a short story or poem about such an experience. It can be true or imaginary. You could make a collage of pictures of such sights instead.

23 The spread of Christianity

Christians are followers of **Jesus Christ** whom they believe to be the Son of God.

Jesus was born into a Jewish family in Israel in about 6 BCE. Little is known about his early life. At about the age of 30 he became a travelling Jewish teacher.

A *Jesus' baptism depicted in a stained glass window*

Before Jesus began his teaching, Christians believe he was **baptized** in the River Jordan (**A**) by a powerful preacher called John. Going into the water was a symbol of a new start (see page 51). John was calling on many people to be baptized in preparation for the coming of the Messiah. The Jews at that time were expecting a king who would set up God's kingdom on earth. Christians believe John recognized that Jesus was the Messiah the Jews were waiting for. The word Messiah is Hebrew for 'anointed' because the kings of Israel were anointed with oil when they were crowned. The Greek word for Messiah is Christ.

Jesus travelled with twelve **disciples**, or followers, and other people who were keen to hear what he had to say. Christians believe he befriended poor and unpopular people and he healed the sick. He taught that God was like a father – loving and forgiving towards all people.

Jesus was not popular with everyone. After he had been teaching for only about three years, his enemies managed to have him killed. He died hanging on a cross. This Roman form of execution is called **crucifixion**.

Jesus' followers believe he rose from the dead (see page 58). They were inspired to carry on teaching his message. The number of followers grew quickly. They became known as Christians. Gradually the teachings of Jesus and his followers were written down. They can be found in what are called the **Gospels** and other books of the Christian **New Testament**. By the middle of the fourth century CE Christianity had spread beyond Israel and could be found in all countries around the Mediterranean Sea. By the late sixth century it had reached Britain.

Christianity continued to spread and develop in different ways. Today it is found in all countries. About a third of the people in the world claim to be Christians. At various times believers have been persecuted for their faith. Right up to the present day, this has helped to strengthen people's faith rather than wipe it out.

Discussion question

Can you suggest why persecution often strengthens people's faith? It is said that indifference (not caring one way or the other) is more of a threat than persecution to the continued growth of Christianity. What do you think about this?

From early times groups of Christians have met together to worship in different ways. The Church now has many different branches or **denominations**.

In the late twentieth century two parts of the world where the Christian religion has grown most rapidly are Africa and Latin America. This means that as Christianity goes into the twenty-first century most of its followers are black (**B**) and the most widely spoken language amongst Christians is Spanish (**C**).

C *The most widely spoken language amongst Christians is Spanish*

B *Black Christians at worship*

THINGS TO DO

1 The Jews were expecting a king who would set up God's kingdom on earth. Jesus did not live the life of a king. Christians believe he was a travelling teacher. However, they also say that he worked to set up the Kingdom of God. What do you think Christians mean by the 'Kingdom of God'? Kings are obviously powerful people but some would say teachers also have great power. Do you agree? In what ways can teachers be said to have power?

2 Christians believe Jesus befriended all sorts of people who were unpopular. Many were the types that others did not want to have anything to do with. Who are the outcasts in our society today? Many Christians believe they should follow Jesus' example in helping such people because God loves everyone. One Christian called Elizabeth said she tries to see Christ in everyone. How do you think this affects her day-to-day life?

3 Christians believe Jesus told his followers to teach about him throughout the world. They believe this is something they should continue to do. In what ways do you think they might set about this task?

4 Are there any ideas or beliefs which are so important to you that you would not give them up at any price? Try to explain why you feel as you do.

Symbols in Christianity

Symbols can be powerful ways of communicating and expressing meaning. They can be words, pictures or actions. The most widely used symbol of Christianity is the **cross** because Jesus died on a cross. This is sometimes a picture or an object. It can also be an action. People make the sign of the cross by touching their forehead, chest, left shoulder and then right.

Some Churches use many symbols in worship. They can help believers concentrate on spiritual things. They help them put everyday concerns out of their minds. In the Orthodox churches there are **icons** (**A**). These are holy pictures of Christ, **Mary** and the saints. **Roman Catholic** churches often have images or statues of Mary and other saints.

Saints are men and women who have dedicated their lives to the service of God. Catholics often light a candle beside the image and say a prayer for someone they love. Some feel they can approach Mary in their everyday prayers because she is the mother of Jesus. They feel she is very close to him and can communicate with him for them.

Some Christians believe that images and symbols distract worshippers. They have little or no decoration in their place of worship. In a **Society of Friends** meeting house, for example, there is no cross and no pictures or images (**B**). There is no written service and no priest, simply a set time and place to be silent and to share thoughts.

Discussion question

Do you think you would prefer a plain or highly decorated place for worship? Why?

A *Orthodox churches are often highly decorated*

B *A Society of Friends meeting house is very simple*

C *Members of the Salvation Army wear a uniform with a badge to show they are Christians*

Many Churches use the symbolic action of breaking of bread and drinking wine. This reminds them of when Jesus did this at the last supper he shared with his friends, the night before he died. In many Churches this will take place at a table. Different Churches call the table by different names: Holy Table, Communion Table, Altar.

Water is a symbol used by many Christian denominations. It is used to welcome people into the Christian family through **baptism**. Some Churches put water in a font to baptize babies. Others, including the Baptist and Pentecostal Churches, do not have **infant baptism** but baptize new believers. These are people who have decided for themselves to live as Christians. They dip their whole body in water (called immersion) to symbolize the end of their old lives and the beginning of a new life with Christ. Some Churches keep Jesus' command to wash each others' feet. This is a sign of humility and service to others.

Many Christians use symbols to let others know they belong to the faith. Members of the **Salvation Army** wear a uniform with a badge (**C**). Others wear a cross or **crucifix** as a necklace, or perhaps a fish brooch or pin. The fish was a secret symbol used by early Christians during a time of persecution. The Greek word for fish is made up of the letters ICTHUS. These were the first letters of the words 'Jesus Christ God's Son Saviour'. Christians understood the meaning of the symbol but their enemies did not.

THINGS TO DO

1 Look at the differences between the two churches in Photos **A** and **B**. Working with a friend, make up a short interview with two Christians from different denominations, explaining the differences between their two places of worship.

2 Why do you think some people choose to use symbols to show they are Christians? Can you think of any difficulties that might arise as a result of making their faith so obvious? Do you wear badges or uniforms to make it clear that you belong to certain groups? How do you feel about this?

3 Christians who are baptized by total immersion make it clear publicly that they intend to live a Christian life. What are the possible advantages and disadvantages of making this decision so public rather than just making a private promise to themselves?

4 Choose some Christian symbols. Make a poster to illustrate and explain them. You might need to find further information in dictionaries, encyclopaedias, CD ROMS and books about Christianity to help you give full explanations.

Adam and Eve

This story is shared by Jews and Christians. Some people believe it to be historically true. Others think it is symbolic. The story is sometimes called 'The Fall'.

God made Adam from the dust of the earth. He breathed life into him and made him a wife, Eve. God prepared a special garden for them called Eden. He put them in the Garden of Eden to care for it. There were trees full of good things to eat. Right in the middle of the garden God put two special trees. One was the Tree of Life and the other was the Tree of Knowledge of Good and Evil. God told Adam and Eve that they could eat the fruit of any tree except the Tree of Knowledge of Good and Evil. If they ate the fruit of that tree, they would die.

The cunning serpent asked Eve which tree God had forbidden them to touch. Eve explained that if they ate from the Tree of Knowledge, they would die. The serpent sneered. Of course they would not die, he said. In fact they would be like gods, knowing the difference between good and evil. Looking at the tree, Eve thought about it. The fruit did look good to eat. So she took some and ate it. She also gave some to Adam. He ate it without question. Suddenly, they saw things differently. For the first time they noticed they were naked. They made clothes out of leaves to cover themselves.

Discussion question

Do you think it is always easy to tell the difference between good and evil? Explain your reasons.

That evening, God was walking in the garden, enjoying the cool air. Adam and Eve hid. God called to them, 'Why are you hiding?' Sheepishly Adam replied, 'I was

A *God cursed the serpent*

naked and afraid so I hid from you.' God asked, 'Who said you were naked? Have you eaten the fruit from the tree that I told you not to eat?'

'The woman made me do it,' Adam complained. Eve, too, passed the blame: 'The serpent tricked me into eating the fruit,' she cried. God was disappointed and angry. He cursed the serpent. It would now always go about on its belly and be an enemy to man and woman (**A**). Woman, too, would suffer as a result of her disobedience. She would experience pain every time she had a child. As for man who had accepted the fruit without question, he would have to earn his bread through endless hard work and effort (**B** and **C**). Neither man nor woman could now escape death. Made from dust they would return to dust.

B *Adam would have to work hard to survive*

To make sure they did not eat the fruit from the Tree of Life as well, God had them turned out of the Garden of Eden. They already knew too much.

C *Man and woman would suffer as a result of their disobedience*

THINGS TO DO

1 In the story of Adam and Eve, man and woman are created perfect in a perfect world. However, they are given the freedom to choose how they will behave. The fact that they chose to disobey God is said to explain why there is suffering and evil in the world made by a God who is perfect. How convincing do you find this explanation? Discuss your ideas in a group. Why do you think people so often choose to do wrong rather than what is good?

2 The story of Adam and Eve is said to explain the origin of **sin**. Christians believe that since then no one has been able to live an entirely good life. Do you think it is impossible to live without doing wrong? Give your reasons.

3 Adam and Eve gave in to temptation. We have all been tempted to do something which we know we should not do. Write a story of your own called 'The Temptation'. It could be an imaginary situation or one you have known.

4 Many Christians believe the meaning of this story is symbolic. Some of the things in it are symbols. Adam could be said to represent all men. What do you think the following things could stand for?
   • Eve
   • The Garden of Eden
   • The Tree of Knowledge.

The Christian Year

The Christian festivals remind believers of the life of Christ. **Christmas** and **Easter** are the most important. However, **Advent**, **Epiphany**, **Lent**, **Ascension Day** and **Pentecost** are also celebrated.

Advent and Lent are both times of preparation: Advent for Christmas and Lent for Easter. These festivals are centred around the main Christian beliefs. It is important for people to get ready in order to understand them fully.

During Advent, Christians prepare their hearts and minds for Christ's coming. They believe that God wanted to show people how much he loved them. So he sent them his most precious gift, his son, to be born on earth. They focus their attention on the story of the birth of Jesus. Wreaths with candles are used to remind people of the coming of Jesus, the 'Light of the World' (**A**).

A *An Advent wreath being lit in church*

Advent means 'coming'. During this time Christians not only remember the story of Jesus' birth. Many also think about his promise to come again at the end of time.

Lent used to be a time of strict fasting and **repentance** (asking forgiveness for wrong-doings). Today many Christians give up something and some still fast. They put themselves to the test. This reminds them of how Jesus did not give in to temptation in the wilderness. During Lent many Christians spend more time than usual in prayer or in the study of their religion.

Discussion question

Fasting is one way of putting yourself to the test. Can you think of times when you have put yourself to the test in some way? Can you explain why you did it and how you felt about it?

The last week of Lent is Holy Week. This reminds Christians of the events of the last week of Jesus' life. Palm Sunday celebrates Jesus riding into Jerusalem on a donkey. Many believed he was the Messiah and greeted him as a king, waving palm branches. Palm crosses are given out in many churches as a reminder. Some organize processions. On Maunday Thursday, Christians remember Jesus' last supper with his disciples when he broke bread and asked them to do this to remember him. He also gave them a new commandment:

'Love one another. As I have loved you, so you must love one another.'

(John 13:34)

In some churches, worshippers feet are washed as a sign of humility and service to others (**B**).

Vigils (times of watchfulness) are held on Thursday evening to remember Jesus praying in the Garden of Gethsemane the night before he died. Good Friday is a very solemn day marking the death of Jesus. Some churches are decorated with purple cloths. Ornaments

B *On Maunday Thursday feet are sometimes washed as a sign of humility and service to others*

may be covered or removed. In many Roman Catholic churches, Christians pray before the **Stations of the Cross**. These are pictures which tell the story of the crucifixion. In some Orthodox churches, the priest carries in an icon of the body of Jesus. People look on as if they were at a funeral.

These and other customs help Christians to think carefully about what Jesus' death means to them: that he died to save the world from sin (**C**).

C *Jesus died to save the world from sin*

THINGS TO DO

1 The custom of Christians washing feet comes from a passage in the Gospel of St John 13:3–17. It describes how Jesus and his disciples were gathered for a meal. Jesus put water in a bowl and washed his disciples' feet. Peter said it was not right for him to do this but Jesus carried on. Afterwards he told his disciples that they should call him Lord and Teacher. He explained that even though he was their teacher it was right for him to wash their feet like a servant. He told them he had given them an example to follow. What does this symbolic action tell us about:
- Jesus
- Peter
- the way Christians are meant to behave towards others?

2 During Advent and Lent many Christians may spend more time than usual in prayer and study of their religion. How do you think this helps them prepare for the festivals of Christmas and Easter? What events or occasions do you prepare for? How do you prepare?

3 Christians are told to love one another as Jesus loves them. In groups discuss what this might mean in practice.

4 Jesus was crucified around the time of the Jewish festival of Pesach (see Unit 14, pages 30–31). The lambs whose blood was used to mark the doorposts of the homes of Israelite slaves in Egypt are called paschal lambs. Work with a partner to try to explain why Jesus is sometimes called the Paschal Lamb.

27

Christmas

Christmas is a time of celebration almost all over the world. For many people it is just a time for the family to get together to exchange presents and share food. People who have no religious faith or are members of faiths other than Christianity share in the festival in this way. For almost all Christians it is a deeply religious occasion.

Discussion question

Why do you think some people who are not Christians celebrate Christmas?

Christmas brings Christians face to face with the belief that God was born into the world in Jesus. This is an idea which many Christians find difficult to understand fully. They call Jesus the 'Son of God'.

The story of Jesus' birth is found in the Gospels of Matthew and Luke. A great many Christians believe they give a true historical record. Others believe the lessons taught by the stories are more important than whether or not they are historically accurate. They tell of Jesus' birth in a stable to ordinary parents. The first people to learn of it were simple shepherds, not grand and important people. When more important people did visit, they were from another country. Christians believe these things mean that God's precious gift was for everyone. They believe that God pays no attention to whether people are rich or poor; grand or not or where they come from.

Jesus taught about God's love for people in a new and fresh way. For this reason he is often called the 'Light of the World'. Christians use lights at Christmas to symbolize this (**A**). However, the lights are not about lighting the darkness of winter. After all, many Christians live where they either do not have seasons or are enjoying summer at this time (**B**). They are there because Jesus lights the way to understanding God.

The Christmas season ends with the feast of Epiphany on 6 January. In the Roman Catholic and **Anglican** Churches this marks the visit of the **magi** or wise men to Jesus with gifts of gold, frankincense and myrrh. In the Orthodox Church, Epiphany is a

A *Christmas tree lights remind Christians that Jesus is the Light of the World*

B *In many countries Christmas is celebrated in the warm summer months*

celebration of three events in the life of Jesus: the visit of the magi, the baptism of Jesus and his first **miracle**. All three events show that Jesus was the Son of God.

Christmas reminds Christians that God showed himself to the world in Jesus. It is now up to them to show God's presence by caring for others and living as Jesus taught them. For this reason many make a special effort to do God's work at Christmas. This might mean singing the message of

C *Christmas is a time when Christians make a special effort to care for others*

Christmas to entertain others, or providing meals and shelter for the poor and homeless (**C**), or a Christmas celebration for the elderly who are alone. It might simply mean renewing their efforts to follow the example of Jesus more closely.

THINGS TO DO

1 Some people complain about Christmas. They say decorations go up too early and that it is just a time for people to make money. Some say it is simply an excuse to over-eat and drink and the real meaning of Christmas has been lost. Discuss these ideas in groups. Each group could prepare a short statement about their views to read to the rest of the class.

2 Epiphany celebrates the visit of the magi. Christians believe they brought gifts to Jesus of gold, frankincense and myrrh. Gold is said to stand for riches and be a gift fit for a king. Frankincense is something which smells sweet when it is burnt. It is used in the worship of God. Myrrh was used in the embalming of dead bodies. Many Christians think these gifts symbolize some of the things they believe about Jesus. What are they? Some Christians say this story may not be historically true but it is still important because it teaches them about who Jesus was. What do you think about this? Discuss your ideas in a group.

3 At Christmas, in particular, Christians try to help and support people who are in need in all sorts of different ways. Choose one of the following to illustrate this:
   • make a collage to illustrate the kinds of help Christians might give
   • produce a church newsletter which explains to members of the church what help will be offered in the community before and around Christmas. The newsletter is trying to persuade people to take part in these activities. You may like to use a computer to help you produce this.

4 Design and explain a symbol which presents Jesus as the Light of the World.

Easter

'Christ is risen'. These are words heard in Christian churches all round the world on Easter morning. In some the decorations and symbolic actions show the joy of this festival. Churches that have been made to look plain during Lent (see pages 54–5) now take the covers off statues. Spring flowers show the belief in new life. Joyful music is heard.

The Orthodox Church has a service very late on Saturday night. It lasts until Sunday morning. Each person in the church has a candle. Candles light the building. At midnight everyone goes outside. The doors are shut leaving the church in complete darkness. This reminds people of Jesus' tomb. Then the priest says, 'Christ is risen,' and as the people reply, 'He is risen indeed,' the church doors are opened. This makes people think of the stone being rolled away from the tomb. Inside all the lights are shining (A).

Christians believe that after he died Jesus came back to life. This is called the **resurrection**. Christians learn about this from stories in the **Bible**. However, at Easter they do not say, 'Christ was risen,' but, 'Christ is risen'. This belief makes a big difference to the way Christians live. They believe Christ is with them today. This does not mean that their lives will be easy or that they will always be happy. Christians will still have problems, difficulties and sadness. The difference is they believe Jesus is with them to help them through. Just as Jesus overcame death so he can help them overcome their problems. This feeling of hope can be found in the lives of many Christians and communities. During the Second World War, for example, the city of Coventry was bombed and its cathedral destroyed. People could have remained bitter and filled with hatred. However, a new cathedral was built. This was a symbol of Christian forgiveness and hope for a new future (**B** and **C**).

A *In the Orthodox Church the church is filled with light early on Easter Saturday*

B *and* **C** *Coventry Cathedral has become a symbol of Christian hope and forgiveness*

When Christians are guided by Jesus, they are setting an example for others and showing God's love. They believe that Jesus can be seen to be alive today in the work and caring of the Christian Church.

Discussion question

The Church is sometimes described as the 'Body of Christ'. Using what you have read so far in this Unit, discuss what you think is meant by this.

Christians believe that by rising to new life Jesus showed there is life after death with God. But because everyone does and thinks things they should not, they could not live with God who is perfect. Christians believe that this problem has been solved because Jesus took away all the sins of the world when he was crucified. The message of Easter is that because Jesus was sacrificed on the cross and rose again, Christians will live a perfect life with God after death.

THINGS TO DO

1 The Resurrection of Christ is a very important Christian belief. Prepare a short radio programme on the subject, along the lines of 'Thought for the Day'.

2 Design an Easter symbol or poster to illustrate Christian beliefs about the death and Resurrection of Christ.

3 Each religion includes beliefs about life after death. What do you think about the Christian idea? What other beliefs about life after death have you heard of? What do you think of these?

4 Read the stories of Jesus' resurrection appearances in Matthew 28, Mark 16:1–18, Luke 24:1–49 and John 20 and 21. Imagine you are a newspaper reporter at the time of Jesus. Write an article which describes the reactions and feelings of some of the people involved. You might like to use a computer to help you do this.

29 Ascension and Pentecost

Christians believe that after Jesus had risen from the dead, he appeared to his disciples and friends several times. On Ascension Day Christians remember when Christ left his followers for the last time to return to God. He commanded them to continue his work on earth. He also promised them the gift of the **Holy Spirit**. The Holy Spirit would be God's presence and power on earth.

The next Christian festival marks the time when the disciples received the Holy Spirit. As the disciples were Jews, they were in Jerusalem to celebrate the festival called Shavuot or Pentecost. It was soon after Jesus' ascension and the disciples, who were lonely and afraid, had gathered together in a room. The story tells of the Spirit coming like a rush of wind and settling like flames on the disciples. After this they found they could speak 'in tongues'. This was a special way of communicating. They were able to speak in languages they had never learnt. They could be understood by all the pilgrims from far off places who had come to Jerusalem for the festival. Many were impressed by what they heard about Jesus and decided to join the disciples. As a sign, they were baptized. This is seen as being the birth, or beginning, of the Christian Church. From this time on Christianity spread rapidly.

In the past, believers were baptized at this time of year. They used to wear white so the day became known as White Sunday. Eventually this became Whitsun.

Exactly what happened to the disciples on this occasion is not clear. However, there is no doubt that they were changed. They had the courage and inspiration to carry on Jesus' teaching. Christians today believe in the power of the Holy Spirit. Many believe God is with them, or even in them, in this form. The Spirit is said to guide the lives of individuals and the work of the whole Church.

A *Worship in a Pentecostal church*

B *Christians use their skills to serve God*

Discussion question

How can Christians tell that it is the Holy Spirit guiding them and not simply their own ideas?

Some Christians still practise speaking in tongues. They allow themselves to be 'moved by the Spirit' and express themselves with shouts of praise (**A**). Others say words and make sounds which do not make sense in the normal way of speaking. This is thought to be a gift of the Holy Spirit. There are many such gifts. Christians believe people are given different talents and skills in order to serve God in a variety of ways. Some gifts may be unusual. Others are far more ordinary but no less important (**B**).

Symbolic words and pictures are used to help to describe or explain the power and inspiration of the Holy Spirit (**C**). At Jesus' baptism the Spirit appeared in the form of a dove. At Pentecost it came as wind and fire. It is also described as life-giving breath.

C *A banner to illustrate Pentecost*

THINGS TO DO

1 St Paul, one of the early Christians, was changed for ever when he believed he met Jesus in some mysterious way on the road to Damascus. Before this he had persecuted Christians. Afterwards, he became a Christian himself and worked hard to spread the Christian message far and wide. (You can read the story in Acts 9:1–19.) Many experiences can change people. Write a story about such an experience. It can be true or imaginary.

2 How do the symbols of wind, breath, fire and a dove help Christians understand what the Holy Spirit is like? Look at Photo **C**. This is a banner in Winchester Cathedral. It is designed to represent Pentecost. How does it illustrate the festival? What do you think about it?

3 Work in a group and discuss what skills and talents members of the group have. How could these gifts be used in the service of God? Present your ideas in a diagram.

4 If Christians believe that God is with them all the time in the form of the Holy Spirit, explain what effect this might have on them.

30 Christian pilgrimage

There are places of Christian pilgrimage in many countries. They are usually where the presence of God has been felt very strongly.

One of the most famous places of pilgrimage is the country of Israel. It was here that Jesus lived, died and, Christians believe, rose again. Large numbers of pilgrims visit places connected with the life of Jesus. At Easter time the city of Jerusalem is of special importance. The 'Via Dolorosa', or 'Way of Sorrow', is very crowded (**A**). It is believed to have been the route Jesus took to the place where he was crucified and then buried. Walking along this route helps some Christians to imagine more clearly what happened to Jesus. They can concentrate on what Jesus' death and Resurrection mean to them.

Discussion question

Some Christians are disappointed to find so many modern buildings and gift shops in the holy places of Israel. Can you suggest why?

The presence of God was also felt in Britain, at Walsingham in Norfolk. In 1061, Lady Richeldis had a vision of the Virgin Mary, the mother of Jesus. She was asked to build a shrine there and a spring of water appeared. A simple building was put up and soon pilgrims began to arrive. Today, about 250,000 people a year visit the Roman Catholic and Anglican chapels there.

In France, Lourdes became a place of pilgrimage in a similar way. Until just over 100 years ago this was an ordinary small town. In 1858 Bernadette Soubirous had visions of the Virgin Mary and a spring of water appeared there. At first no one believed Bernadette's story, but after some time churches were built in the town. Christians started to visit Lourdes and some said that miracles happened there. The spring water is said to have healing powers. Many pilgrims who go to Lourdes are unwell (**B**). Even though few of them are cured of their illnesses, the place seems to give many a feeling of peace. This helps them feel closer to God. Some pilgrims say

A *Pilgrims on the Via Dolorosa*

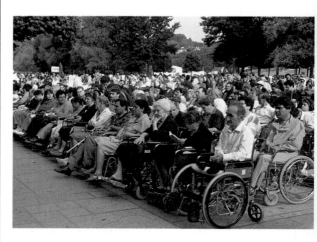

B *Many pilgrims to Lourdes have a feeling of great peace there*

C *The Pope giving his blessing in St Peter's Square, Rome*

that after going to Lourdes they feel stronger inside and this makes their sickness more bearable.

Other towns and cities have become places of pilgrimage because famous Christians have died there. St Peter (one of the **apostles** of Jesus and the first leader of the Christian Church) was put to death in Rome in Italy. His faith in God was so strong that he would rather die than give up teaching the Christian message. His tomb is said to be under the famous St Peter's Church. Many Christians visit this part of Rome. It is called the **Vatican**. It is the centre of the Roman Catholic Church. At festival times, the **Pope**, who is head of the Roman Catholic Church, blesses the large crowds of people who gather in St Peter's Square (**C**).

Many Christians believe that the most important thing about visiting these places of pilgrimage is that the experience can help their faith become stronger and they can come to understand God better.

THINGS TO DO

1 Produce a leaflet advertising an Easter pilgrimage to Israel. Explain where the Christian pilgrims will go and what they might hope to gain from the experience.

2 Many Christians would say it is not the journey or places visited which are the most important things about going on a pilgrimage. It is the spiritual journey that goes on *inside* the pilgrim which is more important. This means their ideas might change or their understanding of Christian beliefs be improved. Try to explain how a time of study, prayer or meditation can be seen as an inner pilgrimage.

3 There are many stories of Jesus and his disciples performing miracles. Many Christians believe miracles still happen. What do you think? Discuss your ideas in a group.

4 St Peter's faith provided an example for Christians to follow. We learn from people we admire. Think of someone you admire. Explain why this person is special and what you have learned from their example or things they have said.

31 Islam: roots and origins

People like to trace their roots and find out about their ancestors and their past. Roots and origins are important in religion too. Each religious tradition tells its own story of the past and points to a plan and purpose in what has happened.

Muslims trace the origins of their religion back to the first human being who they believe was Adam. According to the teachings of **Islam**, Adam was the first man and the first **Muslim**.

The word Islam means peace. Islam also means submission or giving in. A Muslim is someone who submits to the will of **Allah** (**A**). Allah is the Muslim word for God. Muslims believe that everyone is born with free will. Therefore everyone has a choice. One choice is to follow their own path driven by desire, greed and selfishness. Another choice is to submit to the will of Allah and follow the straight path that leads to peace.

Discussion question

Do you believe that we have freedom to choose our own path in life, or is the way decided for us by our background or education or circumstances?

According to the story of Islam, Adam was the first person to submit in obedience and faith to the will of Allah. He was therefore the first Muslim. He was also the first in a line of messengers and prophets (**B**).

A *A Muslim is someone who submits to the will of Allah*

Ādam	*Adam*
Idrīs	*Enoch*
Nūh	*Noah*
Hūd	—
Ṣālih	*Salih*
Ibrāhīm	*Abraham*
Ismā'īl	*Ishmael*
Ishāq	*Isaac*
Lūṭ	*Lot*
Ya'qūb	*Jacob*
Yūsuf	*Joseph*
Shu'aib	—
Ayyūb	*Job*
Mūsā	*Moses*
Hārūn	*Aaron*
Dhū'l-kifl	*Ezekiel*
Dāwūd	*David*
Sulaimān	*Solomon*
Iliās	*Elias*
Al-Yasā'	*Elisha*
Yūnus	*Jonah*
Zakariyyā	*Zechariah*
Yahyā	*John*
'Īsā	*Jesus*
Muhammad	—

B *The prophets and messengers of Allah*

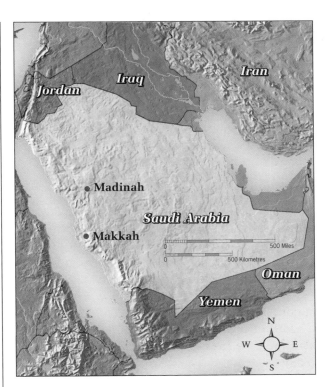

C *Saudi Arabia showing Makkah where Muhammad was born*

According to the teachings of Islam, men and women are not in a position to see what is best for humankind. They are weak and limited in their knowledge. They can only see things from their own point of view. Only Allah is able to judge what path is best for people to follow.

According to Islam, since the beginning of creation, Allah has sent His guidance through prophets and messengers to every nation and every age. He has brought people back to the straight path so they can live in harmony and peace. Sometimes people have forgotten the true message and sometimes it has become distorted or changed. However, Muslims believe that the message of all the prophets and messengers has been one and the same. It is to worship Allah. Allah is the one true God and there is no other god.

The last and final prophet was **Muhammad**. He was born in **Makkah** in what is now Saudi Arabia (**C**). It was here, in the mountains just outside Makkah that Muhammad received the words of the **Qur'an**. Muslims believe the Qur'an contains the word of Allah and that this final **revelation** marks the completion of Allah's message.

THINGS TO DO

1 Draw a diagram to illustrate the two choices that are available to men and women, according to Islam.
2 Draw up a table with two columns. In one column, write down the things you are free to choose in life. In the other, write the things that are decided for you. At the bottom of your columns, write your views on whether or not it is good that some things are decided for you. Explain your answer.
3 Draw a map showing the position of Makkah. Under your map explain why this is an important landmark for Muslims.
4 Muslims look back through history to the messengers Allah has sent to guide people along the right path. Draw up your own list of the important people in your life who have helped to show you the way. Give reasons for your choices.

32 The story of Muhammad

There are many stories about the prophet Muhammad. His life is seen as an example for Muslims to follow. This is the story of how he came to be the messenger and prophet of Allah.

Muhammad was born in 571 CE. His family belonged to one of the powerful Quraish tribes in Makkah. His father died before he was born and his mother died when he was six. The boy Muhammad lived with his grandfather until he was eight. When his grandfather died, he was cared for by his uncle, Abu Talib.

Muhammad looked after his uncle's sheep and later helped in the family business. He became respected and known as trustworthy. A business woman called Khadijah asked him to take charge of her trading company. Under his management the business thrived.

Impressed with his skill and personality, Khadijah proposed marriage and Muhammad accepted. Muhammad and Khadijah became very close.

Muhammad had always thought deeply about life and there were many things that troubled him. He was depressed about the selfishness and corruption around him. The leaders were preoccupied with tribal disputes and power struggles. No one was concerned with the welfare of the poor.

Muhammad was also concerned about religious corruption. The sacred **Ka'bah** (**A**) in Makkah was the place where **Ibrahim** had built the first house dedicated to the worship of God. However, the people no longer worshipped the one true God. Instead they worshipped **idols**.

Discussion question

*What signs of corruption do you think Muhammad would be concerned about if he were alive today (**B**)?*

A *The Ka'bah in Makkah*

B *Do people still ignore the needs of the poor and is there corruption today?*

Muhammad began to spend time in prayer and meditation. He would retreat to a cave on Mount Nur. One day in the month of **Ramadan**, Muhammad was alone in the cave, deep in prayer. The angel Jibril appeared. He commanded Muhammad 'Read.' Muhammad said, 'But I am not a reader.' The angel squeezed him and said again, 'Read!' Once more the answer was, 'But I cannot read.' The angel squeezed him again and commanded him a third time:

'Read in the name of your Lord who created.
Created man from a clot of blood.
Read, your Lord is most Generous.
Who taught by the pen.
Taught man what he did not know.'

(96:1–5)

Muhammad found he did not have to read. He was able to recite the words for they were written on his heart. These were the first words of the Qur'an, the Muslim holy scriptures.

The angel Jibril came with words of revelation for Muhammad many times. Through these revelations Muhammad received the words of the entire Qur'an.

THINGS TO DO

1 A city, a mountain, a cave – these are things you can use to tell the story of Muhammad in words and pictures. You can draw the Ka'bah in Makkah but you must avoid drawing people. Muslims never represent Muhammad in drawings or pictures so as to avoid making idols.

2 Muhammad felt strongly that people should not worship human beings nor things made by human hands. Using pictures from magazines, make a display to illustrate the idols people worship today.

3 Corruption in leadership and the lack of concern for the poor and needy troubled Muhammad deeply. He wanted to make the world a better place. What are the things that trouble you about the world today? How would you go about changing it? Write your answer as a news article.

4 The cave Hira on Mount Nur was a special place for Muhammad. He liked to spend time there. Is there a special place where you like to go? Write a poem or a description about a special place where you go to think and be alone.

33

Signs, symbols and beliefs

Muslims believe in one God, Allah. Allah is Eternal and Absolute and there is none like Him. Belief in the Oneness of Allah is called **tawhid**. Muslims believe that Allah is All-knowing, All-wise and All-powerful. They believe Allah sees all things but no one can see Allah. It is a sin to try to represent Allah in any picture or image. **Mosques** where Muslims worship contain no images. There are no pictures of Muhammad nor any of the prophets. This is to ensure that there is no risk of worshipping idols. Instead of pictures, geometric patterns decorate the building (**A**). Arabic words from the Qur'an are also used as an alternative to pictures.

Allah is merciful, Allah is kind. There are many qualities like these that Muslims use to describe Allah. However, there are no visual symbols to represent these characteristics. Only the words in Arabic which are there to help Muslims remember the 99 beautiful names of Allah.

Muslims have no visual image of Allah. But they do not need it. Allah has revealed everything they need to know about Him in the words of the holy Qur'an. Muslims believe that every word of the Qur'an is the word of Allah (**B**). The Qur'an is a symbol of Allah's great love and kindness towards men and women and it is therefore treated with great respect.

Although images of Allah are forbidden in Islam, signs and symbols are important in Muslim worship. For example, the **mihrab**,

A *Geometric designs and words from the Qur'an are used to decorate the walls of the mosque*

B *The Qur'an contains the words of Allah and is therefore treated with great respect*

C *Muslim prayer positions express humility and obedience*

which is the niche in the wall of the mosque, is a sign of the direction for prayer. All worshippers pray facing towards the holy Ka'bah in Makkah. This is a sign of the unity of Muslims everywhere.

Discussion question

Shared symbols, similar clothes – there are many ways in which groups express their unity and sense of togetherness. What examples can you give?

The Ka'bah is an important symbol for Muslims, reminding them of the faith of Ibrahim. According to the story, Allah tested Ibrahim by asking him to offer his son as a sacrifice. Just as Ibrahim was about to kill the boy, Allah stopped him and provided a ram instead. However, Ibrahim had shown that he was willing to obey Allah. Ibrahim and his son built the Ka'bah and it is therefore a symbol of their perfect faith and obedience.

Washing before prayer, known as **wudu**, is a mark of respect. The positions in which a Muslim prays are signs of faith and submission. Muslims bow right down and put their faces to the ground when they pray. This is a sign of humility and obedience (**C**). At the beginning of their prayer at the mosque Muslims stand shoulder to shoulder – a sign of equality and brotherhood. Everyone is equal before God.

THINGS TO DO

1 Design an information leaflet on the signs and symbols of Islam, using illustrations or diagrams as well as words.
2 The cresent moon is often seen as a symbol for Islam. Some say it is a sign of the lunar calendar which Muslims follow. If you were to choose a symbol to represent perfect faith and obedience what would it be? Draw it and explain your symbol in a paragraph underneath.
3 Design a border made of geometric patterns to go around a piece of written work you are going to do on Islam.
4 If you wanted to encourage a greater sense of equality, friendship and unity in your school, what rules for behaviour and what practices would you introduce? Write an article for a school magazine expressing your ideas.

34

The Creation in Islam

Discussion question

What examples of pattern, purpose and design can you find in nature? Do you think this means that the world is the work of a creator?

Muslims believe that it is possible to see the work of Allah in the world around us. If we look at the sun, the moon, the seasons, the plant and animal worlds, everything works according to a plan. The sun lights the day, the moon serves the night. Spring follows winter and flowers blossom according to their time (**A**). There is no conflict or disorder in the natural world. The Qur'an teaches Muslims that the order, peace and harmony found there is because everything in the natural world has no choice but to obey the will of Allah. Allah created the universe, the world and everything in it and everything follows his law.

A *Spring follows winter and flowers blossom according to their time*

The Qur'an also reminds Muslims that Allah is their creator:

'We have created you from dust, then from a drop of seed, then from a clot, then from a lump of flesh shapely and shapeless.'

(22:5)

Men and women were created by Allah yet in the human world there is conflict and disorder (**B**). This is because men and women were given free will. They can choose to follow or ignore the guidance laid down by Allah.

According to the Qur'an, Adam was the first human being. He learnt to obey the will of Allah. Many hundreds of years after Adam, the earth was full of his descendants. In time they forgot Allah and started to worship idols. They began to lie, cheat and steal, they became greedy and selfish.

Allah sent Nuh, a great prophet, to bring the people back to the straight path. The people did not listen to Nuh and carried on in their misguided ways. Allah asked Nuh to build an ark. Nuh obeyed and set to work. The people laughed and mocked him. Nuh warned them that Allah was going to bring a great flood to cover the whole earth. The people only laughed more.

When the ark was ready, Nuh took one male and one female of each of the animals on the earth. He gathered those men and women who followed the will of Allah and took them on board.

Suddenly the clouds gathered and the rains began to fall. It rained and rained until the earth was covered in water. Every man and woman and every living creature was drowned except for those on board the ark. The floods lasted for five months.

At last the skies began to clear. The ark reached Mount Judi. Nuh and all those on board the ark were able to set foot on dry land. They flourished and followed the will of Allah and the world was at peace again.

B *Refugees flee to safety: it is only in the world of human affairs that there is confusion and disorder*

C *Muslim children learn stories about the prophets*

THINGS TO DO

1 Design a poster that a Muslim school might produce for its younger pupils to show the belief in the peace, order and harmony in nature, and the conflict and disorder in human life. Say how your poster illustrates Muslim beliefs.

2 Tell the story of Nuh in words and pictures. Remember to avoid making any pictures of the prophets. Explain what you think is the meaning of this story at the end.

3 The world after the flood was a perfect world, a new creation. What is your idea of a perfect world? Write a description of it and explain how it would be different from the one we know today.

4 Stories about the prophets help Muslim children learn about the difference between right and wrong (**C**). What stories did you hear when you were young to help you learn about what was right and what was wrong? Tell one of these stories in your own words and explain what it taught you.

35

Ramadan and Id-ul-Fitr

Muslims have a duty to fast for one month every year during Ramadán. This was the month in which Muhammad received the first words of the Qur'an. Islam uses the lunar calendar. This follows the phases of the moon, so the month of Ramadan falls at a different time each year.

During the fast, Muslims must get up before it is light to have their first meal of the day. From the moment a thin line of light appears on the horizon, Muslims have neither food nor drink until it is dark again. Once the sun has gone down, they can break their fast (iftar). They often begin by eating a few dates. In the summer, when the days are long and hot, the fast of Ramadan is very hard.

The very young and the very old do not have to fast. Pregnant women and those who are ill do not do so either. If a Muslim has to miss some days of the fast they can take on extra days of fasting at another time in the year.

There are several reasons for the fast. Going without food reminds Muslims of the hardship of the very poor and they learn what it is like to be hungry. Ramadan is also a time for learning self-discipline. The will of Allah is put before personal wants and needs. By not giving in to the temptations of food, Muslims build up the strength to resist evil in other areas of life.

Discussion question

What is the difference between fasting and dieting?

Ramadan is not dull or gloomy. There is a heightened sense of community because of the shared experience. At this time Muslims try to help one another. They forgive and forget old disagreements. There is more time to go to the mosque, to pray and to study the Qur'an (**A**). Every night when the fast is broken the family meal is like a small celebration (**B**).

Towards the end of the month Muslims go out at night to look for the new moon. The first day of the new month is called

A *Ramadan is a time to study the Qur'an*

B *Every night when the fast is broken the family meal is like a small celebration*

Id-ul-Fitr which means festival of breaking the fast. It is a time of great celebration and thanksgiving. Everyone goes to the mosque for prayers. Families get together for a festive meal and children receive new clothes and presents. At Id-ul-Fitr, the poor are especially remembered and donations are given to those in need. This giving is called **Zakat-ul-Fitr**. Id-ul-Fitr is a time when Muslims are reminded to treat one another as brothers and sisters. So amid the joyful celebrations there is a deep sense of peace.

Fast ends	Fast begins	1997 Jan/Feb	1417 Ramadan	Days
4.13	6.32	10	1	Fri
4.15	6.31	11	2	Sat
4.16	6.31	12	3	Sun
4.18	6.30	13	4	Mon
4.20	6.30	14	5	Tue
4.21	6.29	15	6	Wed
4.23	6.28	16	7	Thur
4.25	6.28	17	8	Fri
4.27	6.27	18	9	Sat
4.28	6.26	19	10	Sun
4.30	6.25	20	11	Mon
4.32	6.24	21	12	Tue
4.34	6.23	22	13	Wed
4.36	6.22	23	14	Thur
4.38	6.21	24	15	Fri
4.39	6.20	25	16	Sat
4.41	6.19	26	17	Sun
4.43	6.18	27	18	Mon
4.45	6.17	28	19	Tue
4.47	6.15	29	20	Wed
4.49	6.14	30	21	Thur
4.51	6.13	31	22	Fri
4.53	6.11	1	23	Sat
4.55	6.10	2	24	Sun
4.57	6.08	3	25	Mon
4.59	6.07	4	26	Tue
5.01	6.05	5	27	Wed
5.03	6.04	6	28	Thur
5.07	6.02	7	29	Fri
5.09	6.01	8	30	Sat

C *A UK timetable for the fast of Ramadan: it reads from right to left*

THINGS TO DO

1 Look at the timetable for Ramadan (**C**). If you were to fast for this month at what time would you have to have breakfast? How many hours would you have to go without food each day? When could you take your evening meal? What problems would you have during this time? Imagine a Muslim friend has written to you asking these questions. Write a letter with your answers.

2 Draw a circle to represent a typical day of Ramadan. Divide the circle into sections to show hours of daylight and hours of darkness. Mark in the times when you would eat if you were fasting. Fill in other things you might do during the day if you were a Muslim keeping the fast; for example, going to the mosque.

3 The month of Ramadan is a time for spiritual and moral growth. Which of the following activities might encourage spiritual or moral growth? List them and explain why you have chosen them. Add other examples of your own:
  • shopping
  • reading poetry
  • listening to music
  • helping someone in need
  • dancing
  • playing cards
  • chatting on the phone
  • singing
  • eating fast food
  • watching TV
  • walking in the countryside.

4 Remembering the hungry is important. Why? How would you encourage people in your school to be more sensitive to the conditions of those in need? Write a script for a role play for use in school worship to raise awareness of the suffering of the poor and hungry.

36

The Hajj

Hajj is the Muslim pilgrimage to Makkah (see map on page 65). A Muslim must make this pilgrimage once in their life if they can afford it. Hajj is a way of showing obedience to Allah. It is an act of worship and it is a very special experience for Muslims.

For Muslims Makkah is a holy city. The Ka'bah in Makkah was first built by Ibrahim. It contains a black stone which Muslims believe was brought by angels from Heaven. At the time of Muhammad the people had forgotten the faith of Ibrahim and worshipped idols. It was Muhammad who re-dedicated the Ka'bah to Allah.

When Muhammad first began to preach many Makkans became Muslims. But the leaders in control of the city did not like Muhammad's influence over the people and he was persecuted. The prophet moved to Madinah where they wanted him to be their leader and so he set up a Muslim community there. To destroy Muslim influence, the Makkans carried out a series of assaults on Madinah. Muhammad had to take action. With an army of 10 000 he entered the holy city of Makkah. The Makkans were unable to put up any resistance. Muhammad declared a peace and forgave the Makkans. The Ka'bah was cleansed of idols and re-dedicated to Allah. Makkah was to become a city of peace.

Discussion question

What would you look for in a city of peace?

Muslims prepare carefully for Hajj. Many have to save for a long time to afford the journey. Before reaching Makkah, pilgrims wash and put on special clothes called **ihram** (**A**). For men this consists of two seamless pieces of white cloth. Women often wear white too. Everyone is dressed the same. This is a sign of equality and oneness.

A *Pilgrims wear ihram as a sign of equality*

B *Pilgrims at the Ka'bah*

The Ka'bah is the first place that Muslims visit on the Hajj. They perform **tawaf** which means walking round the Ka'bah seven times in worship of Allah (**B**). If they are able to get close enough they stop to kiss the black stone. They then go on to visit two hills called Safa and Marwah. According to the Qur'an, Ibrahim's wife Hajar ran between the two hills desperately searching for water for their son, Isma'il. Isma'il scuffed his foot and a spring of water appeared. This spring is called Zamzam.

For the next stage of Hajj, pilgrims travel to Arafat to stand where Muhammad gave his last sermon. The prophet asked Allah to forgive the sins of all believers. At Arafat Muslims stand in silent prayer. They ask for forgiveness and the strength to forgive others. Hajj is a time of peace. Muslims show acts of kindness to one another and there must be no sign of anger or violence.

THINGS TO DO

1 Draw the Ka'bah. Explain why it is an important place for Muslims.
2 Forgiveness is important. It is the beginning of peace, whether in a relationship between individuals or between countries. Write a story about forgiveness to show how important it is.
3 In the desert water marks a special place. For people in many religions, it is a sign of God's goodness. Do you think that people take water for granted? Design a poster or write a poem to draw attention to the wonder of the gift of water.
4 Design and write a postcard a Muslim might send home describing the stages of the journey up to when they reach Arafat. Show how the experience of the Hajj is important or special by the feelings expressed in the writing.

37 Id-ul-Adha

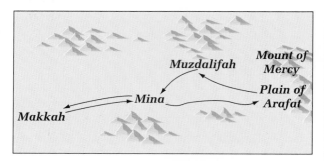

A *The route taken by pilgrims on the Hajj*

The Hajj is made between the eighth and twelfth day of the Islamic month of Dhul-Hijjah, the twelfth month of the Muslim calendar.

There are different stages to the Hajj (**A**), just as there are stages in the journey of faith. At Arafat (**B**), Muslims are reminded of the mercy of Allah and they come away feeling forgiven and at peace with others. The next stage prepares them for going back into the world with all its temptations.

Discussion question

What temptations will Muslims have to face once they return to their lives back home?

At sundown pilgrims travel to Muzdalifah outside Makkah and stay the night there. Before they sleep, pilgrims gather small stones ready for the next day when they go to Mina.

At Mina there are three stone pillars. These represent the powers of **Shaytan**. According to Muslim tradition, it was here that Shaytan tempted Ibrahim and tried to persuade him to ignore Allah. Pilgrims throw their stones at the pillars. This is

B *At Arafat Muslims ask Allah for forgiveness*

C *At Id-ul-Adha some of the meat is shared out. The rest is given to the poor*

symbolic of the need to resist the temptations of Shaytan. Everyone has to struggle to try to overcome evil and temptation in their lives.

After stoning the pillars at Mina, pilgrims wash and cut their hair and dress again in their usual clothes.

The end of the Hajj coincides with the festival of **Id-ul-Adha**. It is the festival of sacrifice. It reminds Muslims of the time when Ibrahim was about to offer his son to be killed as a sacrifice to Allah (see page 69). According to the Qur'an, Allah gave him a ram instead. Id-ul-Adha is a time to remember the faith and obedience of the prophet Ibrahim.

At Id-ul-Adha many families offer a goat or a sheep. The animal is slaughtered according to Islamic food laws. Some of the meat is prepared for a meal which is shared out. The rest is then distributed to the poor (**C**). Muslims must be willing to give up everything for Allah just as Ibrahim was willing to sacrifice his son.

Id-ul-Adha is celebrated by Muslims all over the world and not just by those who are performing Hajj. It is a time for family gatherings, festive food and celebration. The festival is a reminder to Muslims of the importance of putting the will of Allah before their most precious possessions, as Ibrahim put the will of Allah before the love of his own son.

Hajj is a very special and very important religious experience for Muslims. It is an occasion when Muslims can devote every moment of their time to fulfilling the will of Allah.

THINGS TO DO

1 What do you think a Muslim feels about going home after the end of Hajj? Write a diary entry for a Muslim about to leave Mina. Say what has been good, what has been difficult and what they are going to feel when they leave.

2 Draw a map showing the different sites of the Hajj. Draw your own insets from the map to explain the significant points of the journey and the different sacred places to visit.

3 Being willing to give up the most precious thing we have is a hard lesson to learn. Write a story in which someone learns an important lesson from having to give up something they treasure.

4 Muslims call the voice of temptation Shaytan. Prepare a role play in which a person has to choose between right and wrong – where the voice of temptation argues against the voice that is trying to persuade the person to do what is right. Act out your role play to the class and discuss the consequences of the actions in each case.

38

Sikhism: The story of Guru Nanak

Some faiths trace their origins back to a founder or a leader. Others look to a place or a people. **Sikhs** trace their religion back to their founder **Guru Nanak**. They also look to the homeland of their faith which is the Punjab region in northern India (**A**).

Guru Nanak was born in 1469 CE in a small village called Talwandi in the Punjab. It now lies in Pakistan. He was born into a Hindu family. His father worked for a Muslim. At this time Muslims were in power in India but the majority of people were Hindu.

Guru Nanak was an unusual child. He spent much of his time in prayer and meditation. His father had high hopes for his

B *Every day Guru Nanak would spend time in meditation*

future. However, Guru Nanak was more interested in talking with religious teachers and holy men than pursuing a career. He was concerned to see that the religious leaders were not helping the people get closer to God. Instead they made the rules of religion stand in the way of true worship.

Guru Nanak went to live and work in Sultanpur. He did well at his employment and he married and had two sons.

Every day Guru Nanak rose before dawn to bathe in the river. He would then spend time in prayer and meditation (**B**). One morning, Guru Nanak took his usual bath at dawn and he did not reappear. His friends looked everywhere for him. They found his clothes lying on the river bank but no body was found. Three days later Guru Nanak reappeared. Everyone wanted to know where he had been.

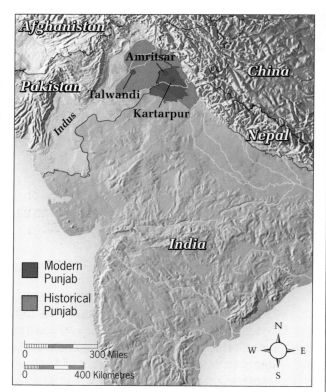

Modern Punjab

Historical Punjab

0   300 Miles
0   400 Kilometres

A *Guru Nanak was born in the Punjab in the north of the Indian subcontinent*

Guru Nanak said he had stood in the presence of God. He had learnt that there was only one truth and that was God. Guru Nanak proclaimed that there was no such thing as a Muslim and no such thing as a Hindu. The truth, he said, was that there was only one God and everyone was equal in the sight of God.

Discussion question

Do you agree with the view that people of different religious traditions are worshipping the same God?

Guru Nanak spent the next 22 years of his life taking God's message to the people. He travelled throughout India and beyond. He was accompanied by two friends, one a musician called Mardana, who was a Muslim by birth. The other was Bala who was a Hindu (**C**). After long years of travelling Guru Nanak returned to the Punjab. He set up a community of followers at Kartarpur. Their way of life was based on devotion to God and the equality of all men and women.

C *Guru Nanak with his friends Mardana and Bala*

THINGS TO DO

1 What were the influences in Guru Nanak's life? Draw a diagram or life map to show the important influences on him and the stages in his life.

2 Do you believe things now that you did not believe before? Have you outgrown some of the beliefs you held in the past? What are the influences in your life that shape the way you think about things? Write your answer in the form of a diary entry.

3 Draw a map of India showing the position of the Punjab. Write a few sentences underneath to say why the Punjab is important for Sikhs.

4 Guru Nanak saw the misery caused by division between people – between men and women and Hindu and Muslim, and between people of different social groups in India. Make a poster to show how divisions between people in the world today still cause misery. In a few sentences to accompany your poster say what you think would be Guru Nanak's message to people today.

39

The Ten Gurus

Stories play an important part in any religion. They keep alive the truths that are central to the faith. The stories about Guru Nanak all illustrate the truth of his teachings.

As Guru Nanak approached death he knew he had to choose a successor to keep alive the message of truth, love and equality. He had two sons. One was a holy man living a life of fasting and meditation alone in the forest, cut off from the real world. The other was a successful businessman totally absorbed in the world of making money.

Guru Nanak taught his followers that the true Sikh should live and work in the world and still love and serve God. So neither of his sons was a suitable model for the way of the Sikh.

Guru Nanak considered many of his followers. Eventually he chose Lehna and gave him a new name, Angad. Ang means 'limb' and Angad means 'from my own body'. Guru Nanak knew that Angad was to be trusted with the task of keeping his followers on the true path. He felt he could leave the world and return to God's presence. The next day Guru Nanak's followers found that he had died.

There was great concern about what to do with Guru Nanak's body. The Muslims wanted to bury the body according to their tradition. The Hindus felt that the body should be cremated in accordance with their religious beliefs. It was suggested that both parties bring flowers to put on either side of the body. Then they should leave and come back the next day. Those whose flowers had remained fresh would be able to take the decision about Guru Nanak's funeral. And so this is what they did.

Discussion question

What do you think that Guru Nanak would have thought about this disagreement between Hindus and Muslims over his funeral?

The next morning when the Muslim and Hindu followers returned the flowers on both sides were fresh. However, there was no body, only the white cloth that had covered it. The two groups divided the cloth, the Muslims buried their half and the Hindus cremated theirs.

A *What is the meaning of the story of the death of Guru Nanak?*

Guru Nanak had nine successors. Together with him they are known as the Ten Gurus of Sikhism (**B**). The word Guru means spiritual or religious leader. They each played a part in laying the foundations of Sikhism. So Sikhs look back to Ten Gurus as the founders of their faith.

Guru Nanak 1469–1539
Guru Angad 1504–52
Guru Amardas 1479–1574
Guru Ram Das 1534–81
Guru Arjan 1563–1606
Guru Har Gobind 1595–1644
Guru Har Rai 1630–61
Guru Har Krishan 1656–64
Guru Tegh Bahadur 1621–75
Guru Gobind Singh 1666–1708

B *The Ten Gurus of Sikhism*

THINGS TO DO

1 What made the two sons of Guru Nanak unsuitable to be Guru Nanak's successor? Design a diagram in words and pictures. Represent the lifestyles of one son on the right and the other on the left. In the centre describe the kind of life that Guru Nanak was looking for in a true Sikh and suitable successor.

2 What are the things that make it difficult for people to live a religious life in the world today? Is it easier to live the religious way of life if you are cut off from the world? Write your answer to these questions in the form of a news article for a Sikh newspaper. End your article with Guru Nanak's teaching on these matters.

3 What do you think is the meaning of the story of Guru Nanak's body? Tell the story in words and pictures and give your explanation of the meaning.

4 Look at the picture of the Ten Gurus (**B**). Founders and leaders are often celebrated in pictures. If you were to make a poster of ten important people who have helped to make the world a better place, who would you put on the poster? Write your answer giving your reasons. Illustrate it if you wish.

40

Symbols and beliefs

Sikhs believe in one God. There are many names to describe God. For example, two that are often used are **Sat Nam**, which means the True Name, and Waheguru, which is translated as Wonderful Lord. Although Sikhs have many names for God, they do not represent God in any picture or image. The basic beliefs about God are summed up in the words of the Mool Mantar (**A**). The Mool Mantar is hard to translate into English because the Sikh concept of God is neither male nor female.

The Mool Mantar
There is one and only One God
Truth is His name
He is the Creator
He is without fear
He is without hate
Immortal
He is beyond birth and death
He is self-illuminated
He is realized by the Grace of the True Guru.

IK ONKAAR   SAT NAAM

KARTA PURKH   NIR BHAU

NIR VAIR   AKAAL MOORAT

AJOONI   SAIBHANG   GUR PARSAAD

A *The Mool Mantar in Punjabi, showing the Ik Onkar symbol*

The symbol **Ik Onkar** (**A**) is sometimes used to represent God. However, there are no images of gods or goddesses in the **gurdwara** – the Sikh place of worship (**B**).

B *There are no images of God in the Sikh place of worship, the gurdwara*

C *The symbol of the khanda*

Another important Sikh symbol is the **khanda (C)**. The sword in the centre symbolizes the One Supreme Truth. The circle around it represents the Infinite and the Absolute for a circle is without beginning or end. The two swords with crossed handles stand for two kinds of strength. On the one hand is spiritual strength and on the other strength to act in the world. A Sikh must be strong in their spiritual life constantly meditating on the name of God. They must also work hard, earn an honest living and be ready to protect the weak and act for the good of others.

Sikhs believe that God created the universe. In the teachings of their scriptures, Sikhs are reminded that God is their creator and that he created everyone. Everyone is a member of God's family and equal in God's eyes. This means that we must be willing to share with others as brothers and sisters and be fair to all people.

Discussion question

Is it important to think about our place in the universe and to see how small our world is? Why do people want to know more about the universe and how it began?

Sikhs believe in reincarnation. Their scriptures teach them that when a person dies the soul survives and is born into a new life and a new body. Sikhs believe that we have all lived many lives before, including animal lives. Being born as a human is an important opportunity to become close to God. Most people are filled with selfish desires and concerns and the Sikh must try to become God-filled. Through prayer and meditation on the name of God the heart and mind can become filled with the awareness of the presence of God. In this way the true Sikh comes close to God.

THINGS TO DO

1 Design a car sticker for Sikhs using the symbols and the words of the Mool Mantar. Write a couple of sentences under your design to explain the meaning of the symbols.
2 Is it hard to keep a balance in life? Do people spend too much time being busy? Do people find time to be still, to reflect on life and its meaning? Design a symbol to represent the importance of balance in life. Explain your symbol in a paragraph.
3 Being filled with selfish desires and concerns is encouraged in our materialistic society. Becoming God-filled is going against the tide. Draw a cartoon strip to compare the life of someone who is filled with selfish desires and concerns and the life of the Sikh who is trying to become God-filled.
4 The existence of God, creation, life and death are all subjects about which all religions have something to say. What are your beliefs concerning these questions? Write a letter to a Sikh friend in which you discuss and compare ideas about them.

41

Symbols in Sikh worship

There are many ways to show that something is very special or important. Often symbols are used to do this. For example, the crown is a symbol of royalty and indicates that a person is important. The candles on a cake are a sign of a special occasion. In their worship, Sikhs show the importance of their holy scriptures by using signs and symbolic actions.

Discussion question

What other examples of symbols can you think of to show that something or someone is important or special?

The Tenth Guru, **Guru Gobind Singh**, proclaimed there would be no further living Guru after his death to guide the Sikh community. Instead, the Sikh scriptures would become the Guru or spiritual guide. The Sikh holy book is called the **Guru Granth Sahib**. It contains the words of Guru Nanak and the teachings of some of his successors. It also contains the words of Hindu and Muslim religious teachers.

The Guru Granth Sahib is treated with great respect (**A**) and shown the same reverence as would be given to a living Guru. In the gurdwara, the Guru Granth Sahib is placed on a raised platform. This is called the **takht**. There is usually a canopy overhead. When the Guru Granth Sahib is in place it looks as if it is on a throne. Embroidered cloths and silks adorn the platform. When the holy book is open a fan

A *The Guru Granth Sahib is treated with great respect*

B *Eating together and sharing food is a powerful symbol of equality*

called a chauri is waved over the pages. This was traditionally used in India as a sign of respect for important people.

When the Guru Granth Sahib is not being used, it is carried to a special room where it rests on a bed. It is then covered with rumalas. These are silken and embroidered cloths that have been donated to the gurdwara by worshippers. The room is usually at the top of the building so that there is no chance of people being able to walk above it.

Food is an important symbol in many religions and it plays a special part in Sikh worship. During the service in the gurdwara, food is offered to the worshippers. This is called **karah parshad** which means blessed food. It symbolizes God's grace and goodness. Every gurdwara has a **langar** or kitchen. This is where food is prepared and served at a community meal after the service (**B**). Sikhs reject the divisions of the Indian society. Eating together and sharing food is a powerful symbol of equality. It is also a way of breaking down barriers and healing divisions between people.

THINGS TO DO

1 Draw the Guru Granth Sahib in position in the gurdwara. Show the takht and the canopy. Label your picture and underneath explain how these signs and symbols express belief and show the importance of the holy scriptures to Sikhs.

2 What objects do you keep in a special place? Perhaps you keep your diary or a very precious gift you have received from someone? Write a letter to a penfriend explaining what this precious object is and why it has to be kept in a special place.

3 What signs or symbols would you use to express the following ideas and beliefs:
   • the equality of all people
   • the belief in reincarnation
   • the importance of sharing?

4 If you were to make a collection of writings that would be important to you what would they be?

42 The Five Ks

The **Five Ks** are important symbols worn by Sikhs who are members of the **Khalsa**. The Khalsa is the community of committed Sikhs who try to live in accordance with the teachings of the Gurus.

Kesh (A), the well-kept, uncut, clean hair of the Sikh is a symbol of commitment and a reminder of the purity and orderliness required in the life of the Sikh. Guru Nanak first started the tradition of keeping the hair in place with the turban. This practice was then taught by all the Gurus. A Sikh should treat his hair as a gift from God. It is therefore important to keep it intact and not to cut it. The hair is a symbol of faith. Keeping long hair represents the acceptance of God's will and so it encourages humility and obedience.

The **kangha** (B) is the small wooden comb. This holds the hair in place. It is a symbol of cleanliness. Just as a comb helps to remove tangles and cleans the hair, so a Sikh is reminded to get rid of any impure thoughts and feelings by repeating the name of God.

Discussion question

The way a person wears their hair is often symbolic or meaningful. What examples of this can you think of, and what is the meaning of the different hairstyles?

The **kara** (B) is the bracelet. It literally means link or bond. It is usually worn on the right wrist. It represents the bond between the Sikh and his or her fellow Sikhs. It also reminds a Sikh of their link with God. The unending circle is a symbol of the unity and

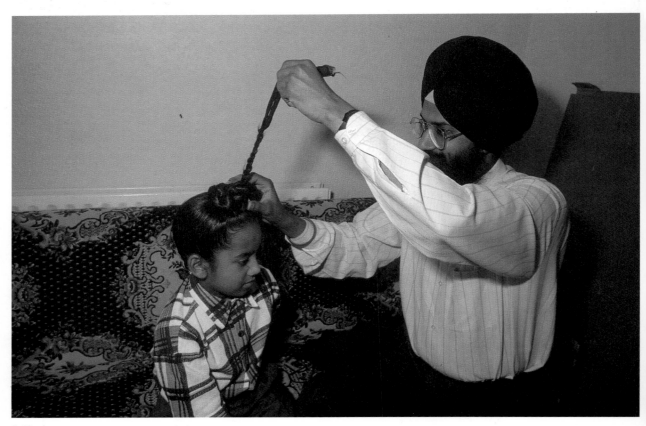

A *Kesh*

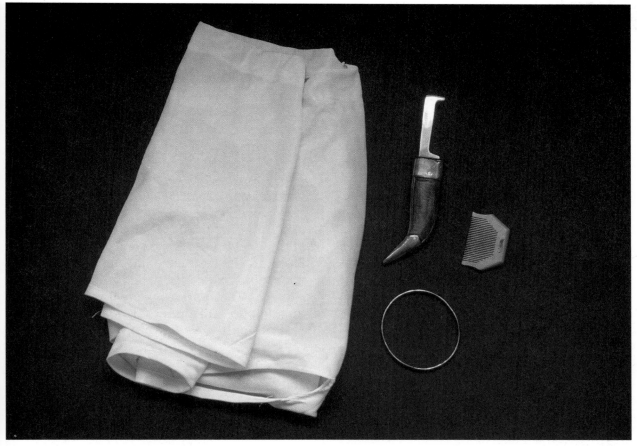

B *Kangha, kara, kachera and kirpan*

eternity of God. It is also a sign of restraint. Sikhs who wear it are constantly reminded in all their actions of the presence of God and the teachings of their faith.

Kachera (B) is the name for the special type of shorts. These replaced the long piece of cloth traditionally worn round the waist in India. Shorts were much easier to move in. They remind the Sikh that they are called to a life of action. They are also a reminder of the importance of purity and self-discipline.

The **kirpan (B)** is the sword. The name comes from the word kirpa and aan. Kirpa means an act of kindness. Aan means honour and self-respect. The kirpan symbolizes strength and freedom of spirit. It is also a mark of dignity and fearlessness in the fight against evil, injustice and oppression.

THINGS TO DO

1 Wearing something keeps it very close to a person. For example, people sometimes wear a locket with a piece of hair or a photo of someone they love. Write a letter from a Sikh to a non-Sikh friend explaining why they wear the Five Ks.

2 Design a poster of the Five Ks. Label the symbols and indicate their meaning.

3 What five important qualities would you look for in a good person; for example, kindness, honesty? Write your answer in full sentences, explaining your choices.

4 Design your own symbols for the five qualities you have chosen in the task above. Draw them and explain how they represent the characteristics you would look for in someone who was good.

Baisakhi

The anniversaries and special days in the course of the Sikh year are called **gurpurbs**. The word means Guru's remembrance day. Some gurpurbs mark the death or martyrdom of one of the Ten Gurus. Others celebrate the birthday of a Guru. For example, many Sikhs celebrate the birthday of Guru Nanak.

Gurpurbs are usually marked by an **Akhand Path**. This is a continuous reading of the Guru Granth Sahib from beginning to end. During the reading, the gurdwara is open 24 hours a day. Worshippers can come and listen and receive karah parshad.

One of the best loved of the Sikh festivals is **Baisakhi**. This marks the birth of the Khalsa

Sikhs – the community of committed Sikhs.

Guru Gobind Singh called all the followers of the Gurus to an assembly at the Indian festival of Baisakhi in 1699. The Sikhs were being persecuted at this time. Guru Gobind Singh warned them that they were going to have to stand up for their faith and even be prepared to give up their lives. He then asked for volunteers who would be willing to face the sword for their faith.

The people sat stunned and silent. No one responded at first. Then one man got up and came forward. Guru Gobind Singh took him into his tent and then came out in front of the crowd with his sword dripping in blood. The Guru asked for another volunteer. Some of the people slipped away. However, another did come forward and then another until there were five willing to give up their lives for the faith. Guru Gobind Singh took each one into the tent and returned with blood on his sword.

A *Guru Gobind Singh with the Panj Piare*

Discussion question

Look at the pictures of Guru Nanak in Unit 38 and Guru Gobind Singh in this Unit. Discuss in class what you think the artists are trying to say about the differences between them and their roles in Sikhism.

Eventually, Guru Gobind Singh came out with all five Sikhs (**A**). He gave them **amrit**, which is water sweetened with sugar. These five became known as the **Panj Piare**, the Pure Ones, and the first members of the Sikh Khalsa. They had a duty to keep a strict code of conduct:

- to follow the teachings of the Gurus
- to offer daily prayers
- to give to charity
- to avoid tobacco and alcohol
- to be faithful in marriage
- to avoid the ritual practices of other religons
- to wear the five Ks.

B *Baisakhi celebrations in the UK*

At Baisakhi everyone tries to be at the gurdwara for the conclusion of the Akand Path. Many Sikhs see the festival as an opportunity to remember the faith of the Panj Piare and to renew their own faith. Everyone gathers for worship at the gurdwara and then all share food in the langar. In some Sikh communities, Baisakhi is celebrated with processions through the streets (**B**).

THINGS TO DO

1 Tell the story of Baisakhi in words and pictures in comic strip form or as a story book for children.

2 Guru Nanak and Guru Gobind Singh represent two important aspects of Sikh life – the spiritual life and the life of action. Write a description of the two Gurus and explain the similarities and differences between them.

3 Draft a letter that a Sikh might write in answer to a non-Sikh friend who has invited them to stay. They have to apologize to say they cannot visit because of Baisakhi. Explain why the occasion is so important and what it means for Sikhs today.

4 Describe a time when you have had to stand up for what you believe, or write a story to show how it is sometimes very important – however difficult – to stand up for your beliefs.

Amritsar

Guru Ram Das was the fourth of the Sikh Gurus. He was a man of great goodness and humility and he based his life on the teachings of Guru Nanak. Men and women came to listen to him teach and to enjoy being in his company.

Guru Ram Das saw the need for a Sikh centre and city. He chose a site in the Punjab region (see page 78) and bought the land. At first he set up a small community. Two pools were dug and a number of small huts were built to house the many followers who visited the Guru. A free langar was also established. In time a small town grew up. This became known as Chak Guru Ram Das.

Guru Ram Das wanted the town to grow and flourish. He encouraged many craftsmen, skilled workers and traders to come and settle. The town grew into a city and became known as Amritsar which means 'pool of nectar'. It was named after the sacred pool which was completed in 1589.

Today the city is a centre of both trade and learning. There are many famous buildings. The most well known is the Golden Temple built by **Guru Arjun** (**A**). Sikhs call it the Darbar Sahib. It stands on an island in the centre of the sacred pool. The outer area of the temple has four entrances. This is to show that people from every corner of the world are welcome. In the centre of the Darbar Sahib, there is a special room where the Guru Granth Sahib is read throughout the day (**B**).

Discussion question

Do you think a religion should open its doors to people, no matter where they come from or what their beliefs are? Or should they require everyone to hold the same religious beliefs?

A *The Golden Temple at Amritsar*

Guru Nanak had taught his followers that it was not necessary to visit holy places to get close to God. He believed it was more important for people to find God in every aspect of their daily lives. Nevertheless, many Sikhs visit the Darbar Sahib. They go to remember the teachings of the Gurus, to listen to the Guru Granth Sahib and to pray. Some bathe in the waters of the sacred pool. Amritsar is a very special place for Sikhs. It is full of the history and tradition of their religion. The art, architecture and the museums attract many tourists as well as the Sikh faithful.

Sikhism has its roots in the Punjab. Many Sikhs now living in the UK have family connections there. When India was separated from what is known as Pakistan, the Sikhs were not consulted and the boundary was drawn right through the Punjab, splitting it in two. Most Sikhs hope that the unity and identity of the Punjab will one day be restored so that once again it can become a homeland for the Sikh community.

B *The Guru Granth Sahib is read in the Golden Temple throughout the day*

THINGS TO DO

1 In words and pictures, tell the story of the development of the holy city of Amritsar in a form that might be used as a teaching aid for Sikh children at the gurdwara.

2 Draw up a list of reasons that a Sikh might give for visiting Amritsar. Use these to develop a script for a radio interview with a Sikh couple who are going to visit the city.

3 If you wanted to set up the ideal community where people lived and worked in harmony, how would you go about it? What would be its aims and rules? How would you encourage the kind of life and fellowship you wanted? Write your answer as an article for a newspaper or magazine.

4 Design a poster made up of words and pictures encouraging Sikhs to visit Amritsar. Include teachings and symbols from the Sikh tradition.

45 Religion and meaning

The six religions introduced in this book have different beliefs and different practices. Although there are some similarities, they use different symbols, tell different stories and celebrate different festivals. Each religion has its own particular view of the world and each offers a different way to travel on the path through life.

Despite these differences, there are some important ways in which the religions are all pulling in the same direction. All of them offer an alternative to a life based on wanting the most money, the newest car, the trendiest clothes, the largest business or the greatest political power. All the faiths encourage people to think about the good of others and to take responsibility for their own actions. They all celebrate truth, love, peace and compassion.

Discussion question

Some people argue that no one religion has access to the whole truth. Do you agree? Can people of different religions learn from each other?

Some people argue that no one religion has a way of getting to the whole truth. It is a bit like the story of the blind men and the elephant. One day a blind man and his blind friends came near to a strange animal. They were told it was an elephant. Each of them wanted to find out just what an elephant was like. The blind men began to touch the animal. The first exclaimed that the elephant was like a pillar. He had only found the animal's leg. The second said it was like a great fan. He had only touched the elephant's ear. The third, fourth and fifth in turn gave their opinions on the matter, having grasped the trunk, the belly and the tail. Of course, they each gave a different version of what an elephant was like. However, none of them gathered the whole truth about the animal.

A *Hindus celebrating God as Mother in the festival of Durga Puja*

B *The symbols of bread and light are important in Christianity*

People of different religions often have very different beliefs about what truth is or the way to get to it. This has been, and often still is, the cause of bitter conflict. However, if religion has sometimes brought out the worst in people it has also often brought out the best. People have been able to change their lives and find meaning and purpose through their religious faith.

Symbols, festivals, journeys and stories are all ways in which religions explore and communicate meaning and truth. In finding out about these expressions of faith, we can look into the ways in which religions respond to the deeper questions of life. We are then in a better position to explore and express our own beliefs.

C *Sikh procession for Guru Nanak's birthday*

THINGS TO DO

1. Draw a diagram or chart to show each religion. Indicate on it some of the symbols, stories and festivals that you have learnt about.
2. Tell your own version of the story about the blind men and the elephant in words and pictures. If you like, you can create a modern-day version. Say what you think the meaning of the story is.
3. Look at the photos in this Unit. Write a set of three questions for two of them. Make sure you know the answers. Swap your questions with a partner and use them as revision aids.
4. Working in a small group, prepare a class presentation on the religion that has most interested you. Say what you think you have learnt from your study of this particular religion.

Glossary

A

Abraham first well known Jewish person. Muslims also respect him as a prophet and a worshipper of Allah

Advent 'coming'. The time of spiritual preparation for Christmas beginning on the fourth Sunday before Christmas (40 days before Christmas in the Eastern Orthodox tradition)

Akhand Path a continuous reading from beginning to end of the Sikh holy scriptures, the Guru Granth Sahib

Allah the Islamic name for God

Amrit blessed water sweetened with sugar used in Sikh ritual

Anglican Churches led by the Archbishop of Canterbury

Apostles followers of Jesus Christ who were sent out to spread his teachings

Arti a welcoming ceremony involving the offering of light

Ascension Day Christian festival celebrating Jesus Christ's last appearance in human form before his ascension into heaven

Aum a sacred sound and symbol representing the infinite

B

Baisakhi a major Sikh festival celebrating the beginning of the Sikh Khalsa

Baptism rite of initiation which involves sprinkling of water or immersion in water

Baptized to have taken part in baptism. Jesus was baptized by immersion in the River Jordan

Bible name given to the holy scriptures of the Christian faith. Jews sometimes use the name to refer to their scriptures too

Blessing gift of happiness

Bodhi tree the tree under which Gotama Buddha achieved enlightenment. It is also known as the Tree of Wisdom

Bodhisattva one who puts off becoming a Buddha in order to help other living beings

Bodhisattva Avalokiteshvara a spiritual being of unending kindness and compassion who helps other beings towards happiness

Brahma Lord of Creation, one of the three main aspects of God

Brahman Supreme Spirit, Universal Spirit, Ultimate Reality, God

Buddha Enlightened Being

Buddhist someone who follows the teachings of Gotama Buddha

C

Canaan the land where the Children of Israel made their home. Jews now call it Israel

Christians people who follow the teachings of Jesus Christ and accept him as God in human form

Christmas festival commemorating the birth of Jesus Christ

Covenant sacred agreement between God and his people

Cross symbol of Christianity and a reminder of the cross on which Jesus Christ died

Crucifix Christian symbol of Jesus Christ on the cross

Crucifixion a method of execution used by the Romans. Criminals were fastened to crosses and left to die

D

Dalai Lama 'Great Ocean'. Spiritual leader of the people of Tibet. He is believed to be a reincarnation of the Bodhisattva Avalokiteshvara

Denominations different branches of the Christian Church

Dhamma the teachings of the Buddha

Dharma duty, law, religion, religious duty

Disciples followers or learners taught by a teacher: in a Christian sense, followers of Jesus Christ

E

Easter main Christian festival celebrating the resurrection of Jesus Christ from the dead

Eightfold Path Gotama Buddha's eight-point guidelines for putting an end to suffering

Elijah a prophet who Jews believe will return before all the people of the world are finally free

Enlightenment liberation from the bonds of earthly life

Epiphany Christian festival which focuses on the visit of the magi to see Jesus Christ

Esala Perahera name given to the Tooth Relic Festival in Kandy, Sri Lanka which takes place in August each year

Exodus the name given to the escape of the Hebrew slaves from Egypt under the leadership of Moses

F

Fasted did not eat or drink

Five Ks five symbols worn by members of the Sikh Khalsa

G

Gentile someone who is not a Jew

Gospels 'good news'. Name given to the books in the Bible which tell the life of Jesus Christ

Gurdwara Sikh place of worship and community centre

Gurpurb special day usually marking the death or an event in the life of one of the Sikh gurus

Guru spiritual teacher, religious teacher

Guru Arjun the fifth of the Ten Gurus of Sikhism

Guru Gobind Singh the last of the Ten Gurus of Sikhism who founded the Khalsa

Guru Granth Sahib the Sikh holy scriptures

Guru Nanak the first of the Ten Gurus of Sikhism, sometimes called the founder of Sikhism

Guru Ram Das the fourth of the Ten Gurus of Sikhism

H

Hagadah 'telling'. A book used at Seder.

Hajj annual pilgrimage to Makkah

Hanukkah 'dedication'. The eight day festival to celebrate the rededication of the Temple by the Maccabees

Hindu someone belonging to the Hindu tradition

Holocaust name given to the suffering of the Jewish people during the Second World War when six million Jews were murdered

Holy Spirit part of the Trinity. God's presence and power in the world, living in Christian believers to guide them

I

Ibrahim the prophet Abraham

Icons paintings of Jesus, Mary and other saints used as an aid to devotion, usually within the Orthodox Church

Idol an object of worship which is only the work of human hands

Id-ul-Adha celebration of the sacrifice or feast of sacrifice

Id-ul-Fitr day of thanksgiving and celebration at the end of the fast of Ramadan

Ihram white cloths worn during Hajj

Ik Onkar There is only One God, the first phrase of the Mool Mantar, a symbol for God

Infant baptism rite of initiation involving sprinkling water on, or immersion in water of infants

Islam submission, peace

Israel the worldwide community of Jews; the land of Israel; and the modern state of Israel founded in 1948

J

Jerusalem holy city in Israel where the Temple, the centre of Jewish worship, used to stand

Jesus Christ the central figure of Christian history. Called the Son of God. With the Father and the Holy Spirit makes up the Trinity – the three aspects of God

Jews people belonging to the faith of Judaism or those born to Jewish mothers

K

Ka'bah the sacred House of God in Makkah

Kachera traditional underwear or shorts. One of the Five Ks

Kangha comb worn in the hair. One of the Five Ks

Kara steel bracelet. One of the Five Ks

Karah parshad blessed food shared out at Sikh worship

Karma actions, the effects and results of actions

Kathina robe giving ceremony for Buddhist monks and nuns

Kesh uncut hair. One of the Five Ks

Khalsa the community of committed Sikhs

Khanda double edged sword used as a symbol in the Sikh Emblem

Kirpan sword worn by members of Sikh Khalsa. One of the Five Ks

Kosher 'fit'. Foods allowed by Jewish dietary laws

Krishna the best loved human form of Lord Vishnu

L

Laity lay people. The ordinary men and women of a religious community who are not priests or monks or nuns

Langar kitchen where food is prepared at the Gurdwara, also means the community meal

Lay ordinary men and women of a religious community who are not priests or monks or nuns

Lent the period leading to Easter

Lotus position name given to the cross-legged position in which the feet rest on the upper surface of the thighs

M

Magi men who came from the east to visit Jesus Christ soon after his birth

Mahayana 'Great Way'. A main form of Buddhism in which belief in Bodhisattvas is important

Makkah (sometimes known as Mecca) the holy city where the Ka'bah is and where Muhammad was born

Mary the mother of Jesus Christ and a Catholic saint

Meditation the control and discipline of the mind which may involve powers of concentration, spending time in deep thought, contemplation, breathing exercises and being still

Merit spiritual reward for certain good works and attitudes

Mezuzah a scroll placed on doorposts of Jewish homes. It contains a section from the Torah and is often placed in a small case

Mihrab niche in mosque wall indicating direction of Makkah

Miracle a wonderful event which cannot be fully explained

Missionaries people sent on a mission, usually to spread religious teachings

Mool Mantar Sikh statement of faith or prayer about God summed up in the words of Guru Nanak

Moses the man who led Hebrew slaves out of Egypt and through the wilderness towards the promised land. It was to Moses that God revealed the Torah

Mosque place of prostration, place of worship

Mudda (or mudra in Sanskrit) a ritual gesture as in the hand positions of Buddha images

Muhammad name of the last of the prophets. Whenever Muslims mention his name they add the words 'peace be upon him'. When written this is sometimes shortened to 'pbuh'

Murti an image of a Hindu god or goddess

Muslim one who submits to the will of Allah

N

New Testament books which, together with the Old Testament (Jewish scriptures), make up the Christian Bible

Nibbana 'blowing out'. A state of perfect peace in which greed, hatred and ignorance are no longer experienced. Buddhist word for liberation from the bonds of earthly life

P

Pali Canon the scriptures used by Theravada Buddhists written in the Pali language

Panj Piare the Five Pure Ones, initiated into the Khalsa by Guru Gobind Singh

Pentecost the Greek name for the Jewish festival of Shavuot which comes seven weeks after Pesach. For Christians it celebrates the day on which the followers of Jesus Christ received the Holy Spirit

Pesach Passover. It is one of the three 'pilgrim' festivals of Judaism. Celebrated in the spring it commemorates the Exodus from Egypt

Pilgrimage a journey with a religious or spiritual purpose or meaning

Pope the head of the Roman Catholic Church, sometimes called the Bishop of Rome

Promised Land the land now known as Israel which Jews believe God promised to Abraham when he made the Covenant with him

Prophet someone sent by God to speak God's message

Puja worship – usually involving offerings at a shrine

Purim a Jewish festival to celebrate the rescue of Jews in Persia. The story is told in the book of Esther.

Pu-Tai name given to the Buddha who will come in the future

Q

Qur'an 'recitation – that which is recited'. The sacred scriptures, Allah's final revelation to humankind

R

Rains retreat a time when Buddhist monks and nuns remain in their own monasteries rather than travelling to teach

Rama one of the human forms of Lord Vishnu

Ramadan the ninth month of the Islamic calendar, during which fasting is required

Rebirth being born into a new life

Reincarnation reborn in another body or form

Relic some item which remains of a person after they have died or something old which serves as a memorial

Repentance to feel sorry for what one has done and willing to start afresh

Resurrection the rising from the dead of Jesus Christ

Revealed shown or given to humankind by God

Revelation something that is revealed, sometimes refers to the words of scripture

Roman Catholic that part of the Christian Church governed by the Bishop of Rome

Rosh Hashanah Jewish New Year

Rupas images of the Buddha

S

Sacrifice an offering of something precious or valued to God

Salvation Army a Christian evangelical church founded by William and Catherine Booth in the nineteenth century

Sangha 'community'. Sometimes the word is used of the community of Buddhist monks (bhikkhus) and nuns (bhikkhunis) and sometimes of the whole Buddhist community

Sat Nam the True Name – one of the titles Sikhs use for God

Seder 'order'. This is a special symbolic meal and retelling of the Exodus from Egypt

Shabbat weekly holy day. It starts at sunset on Friday and ends at nightfall on Saturday

Shavuot Feast of Weeks. It is one of the 'pilgrim' festivals of Judaism and is celebrated seven weeks after Pesach

Shaytan name for Satan or the Devil

Shema an important Jewish prayer from the Torah which expresses a clear belief in one God

Shiva the Lord of Destruction, one of the three main aspects of God

Shofar ram's horn blown at Rosh Hashanah

Shrine a place dedicated to a god or goddess where people worship, usually containing an image

Sikh disciple, one who is seeking the truth

Sin disobedience against the will of God

Society of Friends branch of the Church often known as Quakers

Stations of the Cross pictures which tell the story of Jesus Christ's last hours, his death and entombment

Stupa burial mound

Sukkot one of the three 'pilgrim' festivals of Judaism. It is celebrated in the autumn and is also a harvest festival. The word means 'tabernacles' or 'booths'. These are temporary dwellings built for this festival

Synagogue a Jewish place of meeting, public prayer and study

T

Takht platform on which the Guru Granth Sahib is raised in the Gurdwara

Tallit a four-cornered garment with fringes worn by many Jewish men at some times of prayer

Tawaf the act of walking around the Ka'bah as part of the Hajj

Tawhid belief in the Oneness of Allah

Tefillin small leather boxes containing quotations from the Torah. They are strapped to the forehead and arm for weekday morning prayers

Ten Sayings sometimes Ten Commandments. Ten rules of sayings from the Torah

Theravada 'way of the elders'. A main form of Buddhism developed in Sri Lanka and South East Asia

Three Jewels Buddha, Dhamma and Sangha

Torah law or teaching. The Five Books of Moses

Tzizit fringes of the tallit. It is also the name of the fringed undervest worn by some Jewish men

U

Upanishad one part of the Hindu scriptures

Uposatha days at full moon, new moon and the mid-points of the Buddhist calendar, times of paying special attention to Dhamma

V

Vajrayana a form of Buddhism mainly found in Tibet and India

Varanasi also known as Benares, one of the most famous Hindu places of pilgrimage on the banks of the river Ganges

Vatican the home of the Pope and the centre of the Roman Catholic Church

Vedas the most ancient and sacred of Hindu scriptures

Vigils times of watchfulness

Vishnu the Preserver, one of the three main aspects of God

W

Wesak name of a festival and a month. At this time the birth, enlightenment and passing away of the Buddha are celebrated

Western Buddhist Order a group started by an Englishman in the 1960s to work out a form of Buddhism which is distinctly British

Wudu ritual washing before prayer

Y

Yoga discipline of mind, body and life working towards union with Brahman

Yom Kippur Day of Atonement. This is a day of fasting ten days after Rosh Hashanah

Z

Zakat-ul-Fitr charity-money or other forms of giving to those in need at the end of Ramadan